MARITAL DISCORD AND FAMILY THERAPY

Dr. G Augustine Lourdu

DEDICATION

To all the spouses working tirelessly to find meaning and harmony in their marital lives. Your efforts and resilience are a testament to the power of love and commitment.

CONTENTS

Preface

Marriage is an age-old institution, that has its own responsibilities, bliss, and beauty. But when the ugly side of the marriage encroaches, marital conflict begins into the mind of people. it's an unbearable and inexplicable pain for the spouses, children, relatives and their near and dear ones. We run from pillar to post to explain to the couples to mend their difference, find those similarities between the couple and bear with each other's personality limitation. Couples have been separated for years, without any kind of legal remedy. The children have been tossed between both the parents as they stay apart from each other. As a psychiatric Counsellor, I had the opportunity to counsel spouses in conflict. The families were fragile, some of them experienced abuses in the hands of intimate partner. Couples stayed under one roof because of their children, and to fulfill cultural, social and perception among the community. Separation between couple made the weaker section weaker as she was not welcomed back to her native family or left to live on her own terms. Marriage, marital conflict and discord and its related problems are a vicious circle that extinguishes life itself.

There have been successful stories of reunion, but I must assert that not all reunions are the results of love but they are reunions of compulsion. Social, Economic and cultural compulsions. In a recent event, as a counsellor, I had to deal with the bitter reunion of a separated couple during my marital therapy couple of years ago. The lady in their late 20s was in tears, as she decided to return to her alcoholic and abusive husband, the only reason; she had nowhere else to go or no education to stand on her own feet and she said, "I can't kill myself because I need to take care of my only girl-child". Such painful stories often stir doubts on sanctity of marriage and its cultural practice.

In another example, a husband beat his wife black and blue on the street in a village and no one would dare to go and stop him, because of patriarchal superiority that says that the man can do 'whatever he wants with his spouse'. After the abuse, she rests in her neighbors' house only to return next morning back to her own. Are you shocked by such instances of marital abuse and conflict? This is not rare occurrences but that occurs on a regular basis. 'Stay home and stay safe' was the slogan during Covid 19 lockdown. But for women staying home was not equal to staying safe. The women helpline numbers were over whelmed and there were silent cries were electronically recorded.

Lack of Communication, extra marital affairs, finance, non-cooperation in sex, abuse… can be the triggering factors for marital conflict. There are so many other reasons that was explored through research that is published in this book. "Causes of Marital Conflict and Counselling" is a research work that interviewed over fifty married persons in Chennai, India. The couples hail from a moderately above average socio-economic status. The interview schedule was shared with them and they were asked to identify the causes that lead to marital conflict. Top ten causes of marital causes are also given by the research finding. One of the major findings showed that above 75 per cent of the them do not go to a counsellor because that was a taboo to go to a counsellor for any support.

Do you know when the marital conflicts begin among the couple, is it in the first year of marriage? If you answered 'yes' to that, you are right, because initial conflicts in marriage might increase the bond between the couple but if the conflict continues, it would devastate the marriage and increase psychological and physical distance between couples leading to divorce or outside court settlement.

This book has two parts. Part I explores the concept of family therapy, evolution and history. Complete details of the therapies to be used to children, adults and couples are also given with illustrations and brief explanation. According to research carried out in UK, it states that family therapy is second successful therapy after Cognitive Behavior Therapy (CBT), its right use can actually help families that can build molded and satisfied individual

The second part of the book speaks the causes for marital conflict from minor research carried out by the author himself and gives a template or a framework to solve marital conflict and a few suggestions on how to increase love between couples as well a frame work to rework towards building love and reunion among them. There is no marriage without a flaw but flaws in marriage can be used to enhance their marital bond and understanding. Can we make every marriage work? It is impossible, when they do not work, we need to work towards its resolution, unless after a period of separation the couples still feel, they must separate, we must respect them.

This book is meant for psychiatric social workers, family therapists and psychologists, whose role is to provide therapy and counselling to couples and families who need to resolve their emotional differences and to work with their egos and to deal with *'psychological-dowry'* that they carry from their childhood and their family of origin. Multi-faceted and eclectic approach must be adopted by the therapists understating the culture, tradition, financial status of the family in therapy. The therapist needs to approach the family as a single unit and provide equal opportunity to all to ventilate, analyze, express, decide and resolve about the family as a whole. It's vital that the therapist has a decent knowledge about the different approaches of family therapy from its nativity and modern trends in family therapy as well.

This book could also be used by married couples, the research carried out and causes of marital conflict can throw light and the techniques to improve love in marriage. The couples could discuss the causes and the way to deal with it in a matured and responsible manner and the need to constantly encourage each other in the keeping the flame of love always burning between the couples.

Author name: Dr. G. Augusitne Lourdu

Date 22.05.2024

CHAPTER I

FAMILY, MARRIAGE AND MARITAL CONFLICT

What is a family?

A group of persons united by marriage, or by blood or by adoption and interacting with one another from the respective of social positions and also defined by kinship and blood relationship or through a process of marriage and it's an important social institution that contributes to the growth of the macro society through a well-regulated and empathetic, promotional approach towards early life. These are systems characterized by self-regulation and homeostasis. Every member of the family has a function and by fulfilling the function, s/he maintains balance in a family and the important function in the family is to provide emotional and psychological security.

Modern families are redefining themselves, the significant others become very important to the lives of some people, who are not blood relatives but often part of their lives as the primary caretakers. Due to early childhood experiences of families and dysfunctional nature of the family, in our counselling session, we see that certain blood relatives, or married persons, do not want to have any relationship with their so-called family members. They choose their own significant others in lives and move on as a family unit.

Family members cater to the needs, expectations and problems of each other, experience connectedness between the members and the members believe that they are care takers of each other and stand with each other at all times to build a meaningful relationship and find meaning as well.

Dysfunctional family

Dysfunctional family is that one that experiences conflict, misbehavior, addiction and domestic violence, child abuse, child neglect, mental disorders from the part one of the parents or their children and that occur on a continuously without intervals, the other members of the family are unable to control the behavior or make it a part of the daily routine. Normalizing the dysfunction is the only psychological consolation for the spouse and their children. i.e., For an example, an alcoholic husband regularly abuses his wife continuously and wife begins to feel it's part of marital relationship and she must not take heed to these things as advised by the elders of family in our society. The children are asked not to involve in the conflicts between parents. This is great cause of concern in every society because dysfunctional families not only rob of the 'love and care' for each other, but could create a future of individuals, who experience mental, physical health issues, unable to build meaningful relationship and enjoy decent quality of life for self and others.

Dysfunctional family submerges itself under conflicts, issues and problems, and Conflicts occur due to difference of viewpoints and beliefs between the family members. When the conflicts are continuous in nature, it begins to create a division in marital life.

On the other hand, mental illness of a particular individual too creates incessant family problems as mental health issues are vital component of family dysfunction. Identified patient must be treated on a priority basis and as well work towards family as a system to reformulate family goals in helping the patient as well family must work towards homeostasis. Job loss, academic problems of children, children in conflict with law, inappropriate sexual behavior, sexual dysfunctions, financial problems, extra marital affairs, child abuse and child neglect, remarriage. These issues must be resolved effectively for a purposeful functioning of the family. Dysfunctional family keeps adding to its list conflicts, problems and issues, Indian context, these issues are burdens to be borne by the spouse, children and elderly parents living under one roof. The family constantly battered to the behavior, conflict and issues faced by one or both the parents and creates constant ripples of dysfunction leading to marital breakdown and divorce.

Signs of Family Conflicts

- Frequent argument
- Breakdown in communication
- Disagreement
- Angry outburst
- Avoidance
- physical abuse

Family as a system

Let me begin with a case study, the three-year-old had a terrible accident falling from the stairs, he had a massive head injury resulting in need for complete care. the family was shattered, their schedule was being reorganized. One member of the family had either to quit their job or studies to care for the injured. Dad in the family was working in a private company and the mother was in Government job, the other daughter was studying in school. After various negotiations, the dad decided to quit his job to take care of their son, who was bed ridden due to the injury. He became the primary care giver as the child for the next three years and needed support for his daily routines. The family could not participate in various functions or travel for a vacation. The family experienced fatigue in being imprisoned, after a couple years, the boy succumbed to the injury.

Thus, problems experienced by an individual in a family can lead to financial, social, mental impact on the other members of the family and destabilizes the family as a whole, thus a family functions as a system, when one person is affected, the impact is experienced by all the members, therefore the early sociologists and psychologists always saw, "family as a system, and a systemic approach is needed in the family therapy", was their argument. This is true to all families, addiction, extra marital affairs, marital violence has serious impact on the family as a whole resulting in marital discord and breakdown of families in the society.

Family and Social Role

William Goode defines marital instability as "the failure of one or more individuals to perform their role obligations." And this failure will lead to family discord, but what role obligation everyone has, and who decides that? I think it is decided according to modernization, need and changes of human thinking. I do not want to be on the wrong foot with the modern feminists because the role obligations are changing drastically in the modern society. Both the couple, are home makers and bread winners, or some of the husbands are home makers today, while the wives are bread winners. Whatever the social role and obligations, the family members are called to perfor m in order to keep the unity and bond among the members of the family. In our villages, we often heard complaints from husbands that "the wives, do not cook or care for children", its because of the belief that the women folk must take care of these role obligations as assigned to them by the traditional society. Each society has a prescribed role for every member of the family, and no one gets a job role or job specification as soon the marriage is over or beget your children. Therefore, childhood upbringing, social norms, need of the family decides the role that each member has to play.

Displaced Social Roles

In one of my counselling sessions, 15-year-old boy seemed to make all decision in the family, the father suffered from severe alcoholism and mother was home maker. The boy assumed the role of the "head of the family" and was making decisions for the family. The mother of the family often said, "Now your father is sick, you must take responsibility", the boy had decided to quit his schooling and to work to earn bread for the family. I found this to be an apt example of 'displaced social roles" in the family. We have seen in number of counselling sessions that the roles are often trespassed, tread over but at the end it leads to more chaos within the family. It is important to understand how these social roles are displaced due to incapacity of the key member of the family to perform them. The aim of identifying the displaced social roles is to empower failing member of the family to analyze, how the failure to perform his/her social roles could lead to marital conflict in their family.

It is a common parlance in the villages in India, that young boys leave school to be bread winners to take care other siblings as well as to take care of their ailing or alcoholic parent. Even the girls don the role of primary care takers to the little ones, even when they are as old six. Even though the younger ones take such roles, its still to be researched what happens to the future of this family and serenity of the family must be studied through longitudinal research in order to understand the effect of such a burden of displaced social roles on the shoulders of the young members of the family.

Hollow Marriages

In my own research, I have tried extensively to identify the causes of loveless marriages and also to explore the causes of continuation of some families irrespective of unrest and disorganization. How do we explain that conflict ridden family that are often disorganized do not disintegrate? This conflict-ridden family seems to exist with utmost stubborn from generation to generation. I counselled a family, where conflict, disorganization, addictions have been through the last four generations. the grand parents had marital conflict and lived always apart. The son had perennial problem with his wife, so does the grand son? I am intrigued at this similar pattern of family behaviors between various generations across. This continuation of hollow marriages does not take place in middle class and lower middle-class families, but also among the rich and the affluent in the society.

Early sociologists explained this strange continuation of hollow marriages with system conflict management theory. It means that family is a system that was formed to manage conflicts that arise between its members, when they experience lack of complementarity, unpleasant and repulsive behaviors of the partners. The system conflict management theory states it has to be managed. As in my mini research carried out (%) people believed that marital conflict is 'karma' (fate) and nothing can be done about it but rather just accept the reality and manage the conflicts rather than working to overcome the issues.

I think it's a rather an absurd theory, but the conflict-ridden family and their continuation for generations had the people to believe that managing conflict that arise between family members is the role of family system and in order not to rock the boat or create instability leading to separation or divorce, the members continue to live in the family. In my early experience as a counsellor, there was a chronic alcoholic, who had comorbidities and needed to quit alcohol to live. His post alcohol consumption behavior too was a huge concern for the family, he expressed rage, physical violence, self-harm. The wife with the two little children continued to live with him, every morning she was terrified about the inebriated condition of the husband in the evenings and late night. Eventually after couple of years, the death of the husband brought relief to the family. As she was the bread winner and home maker for the family from the very beginning of marital life.

Family as Interaction

Early sociologists emphasized the interaction theory to explain society and how one understands the other people. This interaction has a serious effect on the mental health of the individual in the family, as longitudinal researches have shown that there is a positive correlation between family interaction, its patterns to psychopathology (Jacob, T. 1987) as well as the mother and child interaction (Zahn-Waxler, C. et.al 2002) and psychopathology. There is a need and a necessity to analyse the interaction patterns between family members in order to see its negative effects on relational and mental health. We can ask the question, what is interaction theory and what are the basic concepts of it? Family interaction approach focuses on the way by which family members actually relate to one another. The family is always seen as a group of interacting personalities. The dynamics in the family could significantly affect the emotional development of a child (Brook et al., 2010). This approach also analyses the parenting styles (which we will discuss later in this book), coping and communication patterns and how it leads to the wholistic growth of a mature individual to deal with the issues of the society today.

In an observational learning of children, it was spotted that parents who involved in physical aggressive behaviors also had children who indulge in physical aggressing behaviors. as one of psychology professor said, "If you have seen your parents fighting, you will fight with your spouse." I find it strange but the interaction patterns (fights/arguments) are often uniform between various generations and the relationship style adopted by you is often similar to that of parenting relationship style. Therefore, family interaction, its relationship style, patterns of communication must be explored during a family therapy session.

Conflicts in Marriage

Conflicts and disagreements are inevitable in every close relationship, including marital relationship. While every marriage relationship is as unique as the individuals it contains, some degree of conflict is actually necessary to keep a marriage dynamic rather than static (Ashford, LeCroy, & Lortie, 2006). Perceptions of marital quality between spouses in conflict vary. Similarly, the approaches which partners take towards handling differences vary but are crucial in determining marital satisfaction. Adjustments can be challenging because it includes adapting to myths and expectations of marriage, learning how to effectively communicate with a spouse, deriving satisfaction from the relationship and learning to deal with conflict. According to Gottman (1994), what is critical in a marriage is a balance between the couple's positive and negative interactions that determines their satisfaction. Studies have shown that failure to do so can bring detrimental effects on the mental health involving both couples and their children. As such, social support measures are extremely vital in buffering the effects of marital conflict.

- Marriage is by nature a multifaceted institution. We define marriage as the emotional and legal commitment of two adults to share emotional and physical intimacy, various tasks, and economic resources.

- Carlfred Broderick 1984, a former president of National council of Family Relations identified nine characteristics to be common across income levels, educational levels, and ethnic groups
  - o Marriage is a demographic event. Each marriage creates a social unit in society.
  - o Marriage is the joining of two family and social networks.
  - o Marriage is a legal contract.
  - o Marriage is an economic union.
  - o Marriage is most common form of adult cohabitation.
  - o Marriage is the context of most human sexual activity.
  - o Marriage is a reproductive unit
  - o Marriage is a unit that socializes the children.
  - o Marriage is the opportunity to develop an intimate, sharing relationship.

Marital Conflict

Buehler et al. (1998) defines marital conflict as the existence of high levels of disagreement, stressful and hostile interactions between spouses, disrespect, and verbal abuse while Cummings (1998) interprets it as "any major or minor interpersonal interaction that involved a difference of opinion, whether it was mostly negative or even mostly positive." Cummings further elaborates that everyday marital conflict refers to daily interactions, whether major or minor, in which couples have a difference of opinion. Thus, everyday marital conflict includes a range of tactical and emotional expressions, both positive and negative. Marital aggression is on the negative extreme of a continuum of marital conflict which includes varying degrees of violent behaviors, including both verbal and physical acts. Definitions of conflict that assume the interdependence of individuals make note of the presence of differences between the two parties. Donohue and Kolt (as cited in Hocker & Wilmont, 1998, p.113) define conflict as "a situation in which interdependent people express (manifest or latent) differences in satisfying their individual needs and interests, and they experience interference from each other in accomplishing these goals". Likewise, Jordan (as cited in Hocker & Wilmont, 1998, p.116) states that "conflict arises when a difference between two or more people necessitates change in at least one person in order for their engagement to continue and develop. The differences cannot coexist without some adjustment".

In sum, based on these definitions, differences between partners may not "coexist" without resolution. It is based on the premise that conflict is an inevitable and valuable aspect of all human association with the use of coercion, including force and violence, as a tactic for resolving conflicts being harmful.

Levels of Marital Conflicts

In a doctoral thesis titled "Levels of marital conflict model: A guide to Assessment and intervention in troubled marriages by Helen Weingarten, M.S.W, PhD identifies five levels of conflict, which has to be recognized by the counsellor in order to help the troubled couples.

1. Problem to solve

2. Disagreement

3. Contest

4. Fight/ flight

5. War

Activity

Couples (Initials)	Level of Conflict	Recent Events	Intervention / Counselling Approaches
	Disagreement	The spouses have adopted opposing positions, marked by frequent emotional outbursts, including crying and anger.	Analysing Issues and Addressing the Emotional Scars They Generate.

Each level of marital conflict signifies escalating dissatisfaction, with higher levels corresponding to increased negative emotions and a greater risk of separation. As conflict levels rise, the gap between spouses widens, reducing the potential for reconciliation or agreement. Family therapists play a crucial role in identifying the level of marital conflict and facilitating its resolution. They employ a variety of counselling approaches tailored to address the unique experiences of each spouse.

Literature on Marital Conflict

It is not new to explore the causes of marital conflicts among the married couples, there has been a long history of empirical research to understand and re-understand the causes of marital conflicts among the couples and their need for social intervention either through counselling or through a social group work. This serious search is a clear sign of commitment to know the reality, as they are, and to show a path way of change to the falling apart married couples. This empirical research, guides the married couples and their counsellors to know their strength and weakness. Review of literature aims to collect various researches carried out at various point of time in history. The past survey and research add strength to this current research to base on a sound foundation of past research.

A Survey found that nearly 40 percent of the 530 participating newlyweds had had at least one "fight" a week, and that nearly 70 percent had had at least one fight a month. Fights lasted from minutes to days; almost two-thirds (63 percent) of the newlyweds checked minutes, another third (33 percent) checked hours, and only 4 percent indicated that their fights lasted days. When a "big conflict" occurred, the styles of resolution varied considerably. The top three approaches were "discussing things calmly" (59 percent) "suffer silently" (41 percent), and "screaming" (47 percent). **(Arond & Paruker 1987)**.

Topic	Per cent
Money	23
Family issues	14
Communication styles	12
Household tasks	12

Personal tastes	11
Decision making	5
Sex	5
Time for each other	5
Value differences	4
Job obligations	3
Religion	2
Friendship	2
Shared interests	1
Marital Goals	1
Total	100

According to a study by Arond and Paruker in 1987, the most common topics of arguments among newlyweds were identified. This research sheds light on the root causes of conflicts in married couples, encompassing issues ranging from financial matters to marital goals.

By the early 1980s, researchers started addressing the limitations of a purely behavioral explanation for marital conflicts. They turned their attention to subjective factors, such as thoughts and feelings, which could influence behavioral interactions or the relationship between behavior and marital satisfaction. For instance, it is now well-documented that interpreting a partner's negative behavior, like coming home late from work or making excuses, in a way that fosters conflict (e.g., "he only thinks about himself and his needs"), rather than in less confrontational ways (e.g., "he was probably stuck in traffic"), is linked to less effective problem-solving, more negative communication during discussions, increased displays of specific negative emotions (e.g., anger, mental or physical distress, and verbal abuse) during problem-solving, and a sharper decline in marital satisfaction over time. These conflict-promoting explanations are also associated with a tendency to reciprocate a partner's negative behavior, regardless of a couple's level of marital satisfaction. Research on these subjective factors, much like observational studies on conflict, has continued to the present day. However, this research signifies an acceptance and expansion of the behavioral approach, which places conflict at the center of understanding marriage (Fincham, 2001)."In contrast, very recently, some investigators have argued that the role of conflict in marriage should be reconsidered. Longitudinal research shows that conflict accounts for a relatively small portion of the variability in later marital outcomes, suggesting that other factors need to be considered in predicting these outcomes **(Karney & Bradbury, 1995)**. In addition, studies have demonstrated a troubling number of "reversal effects" (showing that greater conflict is a predictor of improved marriage; see Fincham & Beach, 1999). It is difficult to account for such findings in a field that, for much of its existence, has focused on providing descriptive data at the expense of building theory.

The sources of conflict within a relationship often evolve over time. Edward Bader and his colleagues collected data on the subjects of couple conflicts over a five-year period. The research began with interviews conducted just before marriage, followed by follow-up interviews at six months, one year, and five years post-marriage.

Before marriage, issues related to the man's job and concerns about time and attention were equally prominent as the leading causes of conflict. Six months after marriage, household tasks became the most common source of conflict, while financial matters came in second place. Issues of time and attention dropped to third place in the hierarchy of conflicts.

At the end of the first year of marriage, household tasks continued to be the top source of conflict, followed by time and attention issues at second place, and handling money conflicts at third place. After five years, household tasks and time and attention issues were tied for first place, while sex had significantly moved up from its thirteenth position to take the third position. The researchers concluded that the most prevalent conflicts among couples were related to the fundamental aspects of living together, such as dividing household chores, managing time and attention, and handling financial matters (Bader, Riddle, & Sinclair, 1981)."

Rethinking the role of conflict also reflects recognition of the fact that most of what we know about conflict behaviour comes from observation of problem-solving discussions and that couples experience verbal problem-solving situations infrequently; about 80% of couples report having overt disagreements once a month or less. As a result, cross-sectional studies of distressed versus non-distressed marriages and longitudinal studies of conflict are being increasingly complemented by research designs that focus on how happy marriages become unhappy.

Finally, there is evidence that marital conflict varies according to contextual factors. For example, diary studies illustrate that couples have more stressful marital interactions at home on days of high general life stress than on other days, and at times and places where they are experiencing multiple competing demands; arguments at work are related to marital arguments, and the occurrence of stressful life events is associated with more conflictual problem-solving discussions.

Marital conflict has been linked to the onset of depressive symptoms, eating disorders, male alcoholism, episodic drinking, binge drinking, and out-of-home drinking. Although married individuals are healthier on average than the unmarried, marital conflict is associated with poorer health and with specific illnesses such as cancer, cardiac disease, and chronic pain, perhaps because hostile behaviours during conflict are related to alterations in immunological, endocrine, and cardiovascular functioning. Physical aggression occurs in about 30 percent of married couples in the United States, leading to significant physical injury in about 10 percent of couples. Marriage is also the most common interpersonal context for homicide, and more women are murdered by their partners than by anyone else. Finally, marital conflict is associated with important family outcomes, including poor parenting, poor adjustment of children, increased likelihood of parent-child conflict, and conflict between siblings. Marital conflicts that are frequent, intense, physical, unresolved, and child related have a particularly negative influence on children, as do marital conflicts that spouses attribute to their child's behavior **(Grych & Fincham, 2001).**

The findings of the extensive literature on marital conflict can be summarized in terms of a simple ratio: The ratio of agreements to disagreements is greater than 1 for happy couples and less than 1 for unhappy couples. Gottman (1993) utilized this ratio to identify couple types. He observed husbands and wives during conversation, recording each spouse's positive and negative behaviors while speaking, and then calculated the cumulative difference between positive and negative behaviours over time for each spouse. Using the patterns in these difference scores, he distinguished regulated couples (increase in positive speaker behaviours relative to negative behaviours' for both spouses over the course of conversation) from nonregulated couples (all other patterns). The regulated couples were more satisfied in their marriage than the nonregulated couples, and also less likely to divorce. Regulated couples displayed positive problem-solving behaviours' and positive affect approximately 5 times as often as negative problem-solving behaviour and negative affect, whereas the corresponding ratio was approximately 1:1 for nonregulated couples.

Interestingly, Gottman's perspective corresponds with the findings of two early, often overlooked studies on the reported frequency of sexual intercourse and of marital arguments **(Howard & Dawes, 1976; Thornton, 1977)**. Both showed that the ratio of sexual intercourse to arguments, rather than their base rates, predicted marital satisfaction.

The environments in which marriages are situated and the intersection between interior processes and external factors that impinge upon marriage are important to consider in painting a more textured picture of marital conflict. This is because problem-solving skills and conflict may have little impact on a marriage in the absence of external stressors. External stressors also may influence marriages directly. In particular, nonmarital stressors may lead to an increased number of negative interactions, as illustrated by the fact that economic stress is associated with marital conflict. There is a growing need to identify the stressors and life events that are and are not influential for different couples and for different stages of marriage, to investigate how these events influence conflict, and to clarify how individuals and marriages may inadvertently generate stressful events. In fact, in considering the ecological niche of the couple (i.e., their life events, family constellation, socioeconomic standing, and stressful circumstances), have recently argued that it may be "at least as important to examine the struggle that exists between the couple . . . and the environment they inhabit as it is to examine the interpersonal struggles that are the focus of our work [observation of conflict]." **(Bradbury, Rogge and Lawrence 2001)**

The assumption that conflict management is the key to successful marriage and that conflict skills can be modified in couple therapy has proved useful in propelling the study of marriage. However, it may have outlived its usefulness, and some researchers are now calling for greater attention to other mechanisms (e.g., spousal social support) that might be responsible for marital outcomes. Indeed, controversy over whether conflict has beneficial or detrimental effects on marriage over time is responsible, in part, for the recent upsurge in longitudinal research on marriage. Notwithstanding diverse opinions on just how central conflict is for understanding marriage, current efforts to study conflict in a broader marital context, which is itself seen as situated in a broader ecological niche, bode well for advancing understanding and leading to more powerful preventive and therapeutic interventions.

Love is not enough to make a successful marriage. The truth of this can be seen in divorce statistics: most people who marry are in love, but roughly half of those who marry divorce. If love at the time of marriage is a poor predictor of marital happiness, what characteristics do predict a happy marriage? Recent studies demonstrate that the type of relationship a couple has before marriage is very predictive of whether they will have a successful and happy marriage.

To identify factors that predict marital satisfaction, two long-term studies of couples were completed. Participating couples were questioned three to four months before their marriage and then followed to a point three to four years after their marriage. Two studies have found that 80 to 85 percent of the time it was possible to predict, on the basis of their prepare inventor scores before marriage, whether a couple would be happily married or divorced. **(Blaine Fowers and David Olson, 1986)**

In a study of wives who perceived that they dominated the marriage, the women had relatively low scores on marital satisfaction. Corrales believed that these wives often exercised power by default, to compensate for a weak or ignoring husband. Husbands in these wife-dominant marriage reported that they were not as dissatisfied with the relationship as their wives were. Kolb and Straus (1974) suggested a "role incapacity" theory to help explain the wives' dissatisfaction. When a man relinquishes his traditional leadership role or fails to carry out his part of an egalitarian relationship, the wife is likely to become dissatisfied because she feels she married a less-than-competent man **(Kolb and Straus, 1974)**

A similar study of the relationship of power to marital satisfaction also revealed wife-dominant relationships to be especially problematic. Raven, Centers, and Rodrigues (1975) found that only 20 percent of the partners in wife-dominated marriages were "very satisfied" with the relationship, whereas more than two-thirds of the partners in other types of power relationship were "very satisfied."

A study among 37 couples measured the power in the family, looking at who made the final decisions and extent to which each spouse had control over the tasks he or she was responsible for. She found that for both husbands and wives, marital satisfaction was statistically related to perceived control over one's tasks. Who performed what task around the house was not as important as having a choice about who performed the tasks? The most satisfying relationship for both the partners was one in which both had equal moderately high control over tasks. **(Madden, 1987)**

In a large-scale study of 5,039 married couples, the researcher looked at the relationship between level of intimacy and satisfaction with marriage. All the couples took a comprehensive marital inventory called ENRICH- containing 10 categories of questions about he issues that are important in a married couple's relationship. The inventory is scored by comparing the responses of the tow partners on all questions in each category, calculating the percentage of agreement for each of the 10 categories, and then averaging the results. The couples with high scores (high percentage of agreement) were identified as high intimacy couples, and those with low scores on the Marital Satisfaction Scale were called low-intimacy couples.

Three important aspects have been found to be very important in building intimacy. They are sexual relationship, communication and conflict resolution. These three areas have been identified repeatedly in various analyses as significant to maintain intimacy in relationship. It is also noteworthy that almost all (86 percent) of the couples in the low-intimacy group had considered divorce. **(Blaine Fowers and David Olson 1989)**

The Janus Report indicated that married couples have higher levels of sexual activity than do divorced persons and that they also have higher levels than single. More specifically, 58 percent of the married couples reported having sexual activity at lease a few times a week, compared with 43 percent for singles and 42 percent for divorced persons. Conversely, only 7 percent of married persons rarely had sex, whereas the figure was 19 percent for singles and 22 percent for divorced persons. In other words, married couples across the life cycle are more active sexually even than singles. (Janus & Janus,1993)

In a survey of 984 mental health professionals (among them, psychologies, psychiatrist, social workers, and marriage and family therapists), one major finding was that 91 percent of those who consulted these professionals said that they felt over stressed at home and in the workplace (Findlay, 1984). More than two-thirds (68 percent) said that these problems had roots in their childhood.

When the respondents listed the most frequent reason their clients cited for seeking therapy, marriage or intimate-relationship were first (78 percent), followed by depression (75 percent), relationship problems with parents, children, or co-workers (70 percent), and self-esteem problems (67 percent). Over half (58 percent) sought treatment due to anxiety; about 40 percent due to alcoholism/drug dependence or personality issues; and a third (32 percent) had sexual problems. **(Findlay, 1984)**

An intensive study of 50 people who divorced looked at which professionals people turned to for help. The most frequent source of professional help for women was clergy, whereas men turned most often to marriage and family therapists. Women were most prone than men to turn to a physician; males and females chose psychologists and psychiatrists about equally. **(Spanier and Thompson, 1984)**

This research examines the happiness of 182 married, urban Hindu husbands and wives. Prior research emphasizes that the processes mediating well-being diverge across cultures with personal desires not impacting the happiness of non-Western couples. However, with globalization as self needs become important, barometers of happiness such as intimacy and conflict in a relationship assume a critical role in the quality and longevity of marriage, even for non-Western marriages in a contemporary India. Participants were 91 Indian couples, married an average of 11 years, from three socioeconomic classes, three family structures, and arranged and love marriages. Results reveal that happy couples, compared with unhappy couples, reported agreement, empathy, validation, support, and fulfilled expectations. Couples' experience and expression of intimacy, affected by social context, also predicted enhanced levels of happiness in marriage while conflict had a negative effect on marital happiness. This research suggests how personal desires may be transforming cultural practices. (http://www.ncbi.nlm.nih.gov/pubmed/19161585)

CHAPTER II

HISTORY OF FAMILY THERAPY

INTRODUCTION

Family is an emotional unit that is maneuvered on the basis of emotional and physical proximity. 'Time to cuddle' both physical and psychological, between the couples, parents and children is an obvious time to experience that attachment, it has a direct consequence on the quality of the future relationship. Families that encourage each other, create a sense of belongingness lead a positive mental health as an individual and in their relationship. A sound family is built on its positive interaction, contribution from every member, family behavior control mechanisms and regular flow of financial support. Thus, a family begins to experience the beauty of being in a family trough a sense of being loved, attached and more over cared by a group of members, who are forever involved in the life of the other.

On the other hand, the initial 'time to cuddle' reduces. Those married couples in the initial stage of love and marriage are always found in the arms of the other, discover the roots of intimacy was just 'sexual instinct' and real love was truly absent between the couples. Various other issues have crapped up the table, making their gap between the couples vivid and the couple could go through five stages according to Helen Weingarten, M.S.W, PhD.

1. Problems to solve
2. Disagreement
3. Contest

4. Fight/ flight

5. War

The marital discord begins with problems to solve, they take about the loss of jobs, financial constraints and problems due to in-laws and other issues. Initially the problems seem solvable, there was always a flood gate of hope that everything will be glorious between the couple, that the sweet bitter time was mixed happy tears between the couple. But when the problems seem to be perennial, the couples begin to lose their patience and begin a cold war of disagreement and contest one another's point of view.

This is another important stage of family conflict, in which, the decision to separate and divorce begin to set in. the couples mull on the idea of freeing themselves from the clutches of the imprisoned marital chains. The fight or flight mode is activated, there begins a triangulation (involvement of the third person) be introduced, be it a good friend or a family member, counselor between the couples. The last resort is 'war'. They begin to plot against each other, making the marital life a hell on earth and constant verbal physical, psychological torture being shared between the couples.

Can you imagine the experience of children during these five stages of marital discord? The couples will make use of the children to prove their points, garner support from the kids to malign the name of the partner among family and friends or in the court of law. Have we not heard of cases, in which the mother, accused the husband of sexually abusing their own daughter, but later the truth was the daughter was coerced by the mother to lie about her biological father? What a relief for the male parent, yet 'war' could break loose in the marital discord. In Indian context, some call marital union as a 'life-time imprisonment' on a lighter note, yet for people, with personality differences, psychiatric and other issues could truly be a 'life-time imprisonment'.

All of us have been in a family, and as a child we have seen the conflict between our parents, the intervention of a third person. We have experienced financial, verbal, physical, sexual deprivations and often felt isolated, unloved due to faulty parenting, over concerned and over protective or domineering, violent parenting. I strongly believe that makes us vulnerable. Our individual life and relational life will be affected by the experience of the family because an individual is a product of a family, his present and future self, neuroticism as well as psychotic behavior patterns of the experience in the family. Thus, the role of family therapy comes into play. A form of psychotherapy, in the words of Sigmund Freud, "Child is the father of man". The causes of marital discord must be seen through the early childhood experiences, and to finish the 'unfinished businesses' of the early childhood and the experiences that are imprinted and cause the primal pain that all members experience.

Before we begin to explore the meaning of family therapy, let us explore another important concept of self. The concept of self is a vital concept in 'psycho analytical theory', there is a general consensus that the development of the self is a result within the context of certain key relationships. As Benjamin, (1988) states that "we grow out of relationships rather than becoming more active and sovereign within them", Mahler et al. (1975) in a research state that the healthy concept of self is a result of a linear progression of caregiver-infant relationship. Bowen (1989) believed that there is a similar pattern of behavior between the three generations and all neurotic and behavioral patterns are a result of the early experience among the key relationships, the care givers. The family therapy will explore the possibility of the self as a hindering factor in autonomous and relational self. Most often the marital discord begins with the 'problem of the self', 'problem of habits.' Therefore, an individual must work with his own 'concept of self' before exploring the issues of relationship, marital discord and other factors.

Definition and Meaning of Family Therapy

Family therapy is a type of psychotherapy that involves all members of a nuclear family or stepfamily and, in some cases, members of the extended family (e.g., grandparents). A therapist or team of therapists conducts multiple sessions to help families deal with important issues that may interfere with the functioning of the family and the home environment. There are many definitions and explanations that are given for family therapy, let's explore some of them here for our understanding.

The Wikipedia defines, "Family therapy, also referred to as couple and family therapy, marriage and family therapy, family systems therapy, and family counselling, is a branch of psychology that works with families and couples in intimate relationship to nurture change and development". (https://en.wikipedia.org/wiki/Family_therapy).

Family therapy can be defined as a, "process that revisits the goals, roles, interactions in a systemic approach and to identify and address issues that affect psychological, relational health of a family and it make use of family therapy techniques as a primary mode of treatment."

The family therapy also works with communication styles and patterns between the family members to understand the causes of conflicts. It includes all the members of the family, who experience family discord and conflict due to various issues. As Bowen, rightly points out that three generations often have similar personality traits as well as behaviors patterns, communication styles and analyzing the three generation can throw light in the treatment process of a family.

As a family therapist and counsellor, I have found that family therapy is an all-encompassing experience for both the members of the family and the therapists because the whole discussion has a past, present and a future. It has got great moment of love experience, worst experience of rejection. There is also a great fear of how the 'community looks at my family' especially in Indian village setting. There is a constant effort to placard to other members of the community that 'all is well' in my family. There are high frequency arguments, domestic violence, helpless children observing without understanding. Therefore, I consider that family therapy is a drama of all dramas in real life.

Let us discuss the contribution of various authors in making the family therapy a reality and to discuss a couple of family therapies that can actually help psychologists and Psychiatric social workers in counselling families and to create strategies to improve family living and also to build tools for family therapy.

Evolution of Family Therapy

The end of World War II and the soldiers returned to their families in an atmosphere of emotional, psychological and physical deprivation. They experienced so much of violence and war crimes during the unspeakable nature of war and lack of accountability regarding war crimes during those times. The soldiers back home had to adjust with the normal society, women have joined the work force due to the absence of their husband due to their duties at war. Working women, exposure to violence during war for the husbands began upsetting the whole functioning of family. The families began to experience psychological imbalance, outburst and often let to domestic, physical and sexual abuse in in 1950's. During those years, psychotherapy was very popular among psychological practitioners, these professionals were now expected to work effectively with an array of problems within the family. World war taught them to look at the way of making our psychological and family life by understanding the family form a system perspective that in turn gave birth to family psychotherapy.

Early Contribution to family therapy

- Family dynamics and adult psychopathology was analyzed. Various research showed there has been a positive correlation between the family dynamics and adult psychopathology.

- The role of the family was investigated in the development schizophrenia of one of its members. In research by Frieda Fromm-Reichmann (1948) postulated that maternal rejection led to schizophrenia among the males. It was identified that a there was a cause-and-effect relationship between pathogenic parents and Schizophrenia. Yet the question of nature V/s nurture comes into play among the modern therapists. Therefore, the early study of maternal rejection and schizophrenia was rejected by the future researchers. This led to pave a way for the role of family in psychopathology and other personality disorder in an individual. I would argue that the rejection of any correlation between schizophrenia and maternal rejection has pioneered more research into family dynamics, family interaction, family discord and conflict and its effect on the psychological health of every individual member in the family.

Another research that was carried out to study the communication patterns and paradoxes in the year 1952. The research group began to study the possible link between pathological communication patterns within a family and the emergence and maintenance of the schizophrenic behaviors in a family member. One of the intriguing findings was that the schizophrenic sent often conflicting and contradictory feedback messages at the same time. These researchers also showed that schizophrenics often withdraw from the world of relationship as they see the pathological communication patterns and paradoxes have led to distrust in the family life and the world as a whole. It is important to note that the 'deterministic theory' of

Sigmund Freud that the childhood pathological interaction will continue to haunt the adult life and its relationship is worth recalling. Thus, the researchers have found that that schizophrenia as a prototype of the consequence of failure in a family's communication system.

At the same time, Theodore litz, began another important research from John Hopkins University in 1960s. He rejected the idea of rejecting-mother as a contributing factor to pathology but the role of the father and the possibility of the destructive role. He identified the following five pathological patterns of fathering. The role of the father was first studies to identify the problems faced by the later adults as well as the family conflicts.

1. Rigid and Domineering
2. Hostile
3. Paranoid
4. Little or no consequence at home
5. Passive and submissive

These patterns had been experienced by schizophrenic patients. Even though we know that Schizophrenia is a genetic and biological issues, yet it has it has a triggering point on the destructive role the father has played during the early childhood and initial stage of the marriage.

Chronic family discord was also found to be another causative factor to the early onset of schizophrenia. When there is continuous discord, each of the parent, is often worried about their own problems and issues and fails to play the role that is given to him by the family or one of the spouses carries out the responsibility and the other is mute spectator in the family, who is overburdened with his own personal problems. This leads to lack of participation in family activities and leads to reduction in physical proximity, sexual intimacy and later loss of love and emotional attachment with the family leading to family conflict and marital discord. If the roles are not played by the spouses, eventually there will be a day, when divorce will be inevitable.

Bowen, one of the founders of family therapy, had interesting research and continued on the chronic family discord and the maternal-rejection of the early researches. Bowen called the emotional distance between the parents and the schizophrenic patients as 'emotional divorce'. Even though the child, who was physically attached to the parents in the early stages of childhood, s/he begins to seek autonomy in the being of adolescent, this could be a typical time of onset for schizophrenia asserted by the research. He suggested that the 'three generation theory' that schizophrenia is a process that spans for the three generation and calls to study the generation as they have common patterns of communication i.e., positive or pathological. The parent, who has experienced serious emotional conflict by their parents, often want to subject their child children with the same serious emotional conflict. Therefore, passed the deficit of the family in its interaction, relationship to the next generation, making the generation vulnerable and unable to build health family and enhanced self.

- The historical roots and development of Marital counselling began.
- The earliest development of Child and adolescents' guidance movement emphasizing the role of the family in helping process. Adler…
- There was also growth in group therapy, in which the family was considered as a group yet a single unit, any disorder with one members of the family can actually infringe negativity to that unit. The therapists considered the family as an emotion unit, in which every member played an important role to the homeostasis, if one of the members actually tilted this unit, the whole unit will suffer and bring about discord among the family members.

Family Therapy in India

The family therapy officially entered India in the 1970s with the establishment of Family psychiatric Centre at the National Institute of Mental Health and Neuroscience in Bangalore. (NIMHANS). The Centre offered a three-month orientation courses in integrative systemic family therapy. There are other professional began to explore various other techniques of family therapy, including theory, case study and role play. In the year, 1994, Indian Association of Family therapy (IAFT) was established formally. The initially the family therapists were trained by experts from the West and many experts wish a unique and India way of administering family therapy.

Different schools of social work are offering family therapy as an academic subject as well encourage experts to practice in India. The courts have even opened counselling centers for spouses with marital conflict.

- India lives in extended and joint families. The culture and its compulsions have made it difficult to reach out for family therapies. The unwritten norms and taboo related to speaking about marital discord, or the personality or behavior of the spouse is considered as 'washing the dirty linen in the public', The couples in India, would like to paint a rosy picture about their family to their other members of the family and neighbors and friends. Bur the truth is, the simmering about their families and the roles they have to play continues to haunt them in their heart. In a book, written by R.K. Narayan, 'The Dark Room', he pens the harsh abuses experienced by the protagonist 'Savitri', who experiences harsh abuses under the rigid traditional values. Savitri uses the dark room in her house after a long hours of household chores to CRY. The dark room is the reality in Indian context, even women are found crying in day light too.

- In my mini research, the data showed that about 75 per cent of respondents felt that its taboo to seek help in a metro city of India. They also believed that its their 'fate' or 'karma' in Indian traditional misguided belief of predestination. This is not going to be an easy ride for the counsellors to take the couple through family therapy and make it an effective tool to enhance communication and as well as to improve healthy marital relationship;

- Review of literature on Family therapy supports that systemic thinking, which deals with pattern of relationships, is valid for all families regardless of cultural differences (Tamura and Lau, 1992). Systemic thinking and triangulation would appear to be a suitable form of intervention for families in India. Traditionally, individual is a part of the family and family takes care of the individual through all his struggles and problems.

Who are not considered for Family therapy?

- If one or more members of the family have psychotic or serious mental illness.
- If there is unwillingness from the part of the family members
- One who has rigid personality and unwilling to cooperate during session after considerable days of therapy.
- If they do not live together or meet each other.

Goals of Family Therapy

Exploring Family Dynamics: Family therapy aims to delve into the dynamics of family interactions and relationships. This includes an examination of parenting styles and an understanding of the couple's history, which can provide valuable insights into the family's current challenges.

Psychoeducation: Providing psychoeducation to the family involves offering information and knowledge to help them better understand their issues. It can include teaching them about mental health, communication, conflict resolution, and other relevant topics to enhance their awareness and coping skills.

Empowerment and Ego Strength: Family therapy aims to empower family members by increasing their self-esteem and ego strength. This involves building their confidence and resilience, which can be essential for coping with family challenges.

Improving Communication: Effective communication is a key goal of family therapy. It seeks to enhance the way family members communicate with each other, fostering more open, respectful, and constructive dialogue.

Modifying Interaction Patterns: The therapy seeks to modify existing interaction patterns within the family. This can involve identifying and changing negative patterns and replacing them with healthier and more adaptive ones.

Reframing Relationships: The goal of family therapy is to help family members reframe their relationships and interactions in a way that promotes a more adaptive and harmonious family life. It may involve shifting perspectives and adopting healthier attitudes toward one another.

These goals collectively work towards enhancing the overall functioning and well-being of the family, fostering more positive and supportive relationships among its members. Family therapy can be a valuable resource for families facing challenges, providing them with the tools and insights needed to work through their issues effectively.

Stages in Family therapy

Stages in family therapy must be founded on comprehensive psychological theories and models because they help us to navigate a course of action or justify the action and to diagnose the deep-rooted issues that are experienced by a family. The various schools/models of family therapy (discussed in the book) identify the causes of marital discord and the steps in creating a treatment plan and to reframe dynamics of communication, interaction and relationship. It demands for a deeper investigation into three generations, Family history, family illness and as well as its dynamics. Each stage must be comprehensively understood and analyzed. This comprehensive foundation provides structure and evidence-based guidance for family therapists to work with families, addressing their unique challenges and facilitating positive change.

1. The referral and Intake
2. The Assessment stages
3. The treatment plan stage
4. Short term goals assessment stage
5. Long term goals planning stage
6. Termination

Case Example 1

Savitri (name changed) has been married for the past 14 years and is the mother of three children. Unfortunately, she finds herself in a difficult situation with an abusive and alcoholic husband. His excessive drinking leads to frequent incidents of physical violence. Despite the challenges, Savitri works in a garment factory to provide for her family. She not only takes care of the children but also manages the financial responsibilities, including paying off debts that the family has accrued for various reasons. Savitri's resilience is remarkable, but she often suffers from physical wounds and pain on her back due to the abuse by her husband. In light of these circumstances, the family of five sought help through family therapy, recognizing the need for support and intervention.

Therapeutic approaches

Externalization Technique: This technique was used to separate the problem from the client, helping to improve the client's self-esteem. By externalizing the issue, individuals can view it more objectively and reduce the emotional burden it carries.

Dealing with Addiction: Addiction was identified as a triggering point for the family's problems. The therapist assisted the client in seeking deaddiction support, including joining an AA (Alcoholics Anonymous) group and obtaining a sponsor to aid in maintaining sobriety. Addressing the addiction issue is often a crucial step in family therapy.

Narrative Therapy: This approach and its techniques were used to reduce emotional turmoil and help family members differentiate between their thoughts and feelings. Narrative therapy can be effective in reframing and restructuring the stories individuals tell themselves about their experiences.

Reversal of Role Technique: This technique was implemented with the clients, allowing them to explore and understand different perspectives by temporarily assuming roles or viewpoints within the family.

Visualization Technique: The family was encouraged to visualize their desired family dynamic and functioning. They were given the opportunity to express their visions and contributions, ultimately creating a timeline to work toward the visualized family goal. Visualization can be a powerful tool for setting and achieving shared family objectives.

These techniques collectively supported the family in addressing their challenges, improving communication and relationships, and working toward a healthier and more functional family unit.

Outcome

1. **Love Banks Between Couples:** The use of "Love Banks" is a method to encourage the exchange of love and affection between couples. This technique helps to enhance the emotional connection and intimacy in the marital relationship.

2. **"Thank You" Notes:** The practice of writing and exchanging "Thank You" notes among the children was implemented. This technique promotes gratitude and positive interactions within the family, strengthening bonds between family members.

3. **Family Meetings:** Regular family meetings were held, providing a platform for open communication and discussion. These meetings allowed family members to share their thoughts, concerns, and achievements, fostering a sense of unity and understanding.

4. **Family Meals:** The increase in family meals is another positive step. Sharing meals together not only encourages healthy eating habits but also strengthens the family bond through shared experiences and conversations.

These techniques and strategies helped the family improve their dynamics, increase positive interactions, and work together to achieve their goals. It's evident that the family was committed to positive change and building a healthier, more connected family unit.

Case Example 2

Rani, in her 30s and married for 15 years with four children, faced a challenging situation with her mental health. Her initial experience of depression after the tragic loss of her parents led to a diagnosis of paranoid schizophrenia. Despite having a supportive husband with a good income, Rani struggled with persistent paranoia and suspicion regarding his behavior. She displayed frequent temper tantrums in the presence of family members and relatives, neglected self-care, refused to eat food prepared by others, and experienced hallucinations and delusions. This illness took a toll on the entire family, with the children bearing the brunt of her condition. To manage her violent episodes and delusions, the family felt compelled to isolate themselves, resulting in a challenging and distressing situation for everyone involved.

Analysis

In the challenging situation where the mother was unable to actively participate in family therapy due to her psychotic symptoms and illness, the head of the family took the initiative to seek support and understanding for the family. While traditional family therapy may not have been possible, a counselling session was conducted for the family members. During this process:

1. **Initiative of the Head of the Family:** The head of the family played a crucial role in bringing the children and grandparents into the counselling process. This proactive approach aimed to help them understand and cope with the mental illness of the wife and mother while maintaining the family's unity and spirit.

2. **Constructing and Deconstructing Experiences:** The children were encouraged to construct and deconstruct their own experiences, feelings, and perspectives. This process allowed them to explore and express their emotions, fears, and hopes in response to the challenges they were facing as a family.

3. **Narrative Therapy Techniques:** The therapist used narrative therapy techniques to read between the lines of the family's problem story. This approach helps uncover hidden narratives and perspectives, enabling the family to reframe their experiences and develop a more empowering narrative.

4. **Family as Part of the Recovery Process:** Recognizing the importance of family in the recovery process for the mother, the counselling session included the family members as active participants in supporting her. Their understanding and coping strategies could play a significant role in her healing journey.

This approach demonstrates the family's resilience and determination to work together to address the impact of mental illness on their lives and maintain their bonds despite the challenges they face.

Outcome

It's heartening to hear that the family made significant improvements in their communication and relationships. Their decision to come together and focus on the mother's mental illness is a positive step. By actively participating in her recovery process and offering support and understanding, the family can play a pivotal role in her healing journey. Their commitment to working as a united front in the face of challenges demonstrates their strength and resilience as a family.

CHAPTER III

SCHOOLS OF FAMILY THERAPY

PSYCHODYNAMIC MODEL

I have been influenced by the work of Dr. Sigmund Freud and the psychodynamic approach to psychotherapy. Freud's contributions to the field of psychology have had a profound impact on our understanding of the human mind and behavior. The psychodynamic approach, with its focus on exploring past experiences and their impact on emotions, thoughts, and beliefs, is a fundamental aspect of Freudian psychoanalysis.

1. **Patterns and Past Experiences:** The psychodynamic approach aims to identify patterns in a client's past experiences and how these patterns influence their current emotions, thoughts, and beliefs. These patterns often result from unresolved issues from childhood.

2. **Primal Pain and the Inner Child:** "Primal Pain" and the idea of healing the inner child. This is a perspective within psychodynamic therapy that suggests individuals carry unmet needs, desires, or emotional wounds from their early years, which continue to impact their lives.

3. **Unconscious Roots of Chronic Problems:** The psychodynamic approach asserts that many chronic problems have their roots in the unconscious mind. These issues may not be readily apparent to the individual but can be brought to light through the process of catharsis, which involves the release of pent-up emotions and emotional healing.

The psychodynamic approach, while historically significant, is one of several therapeutic approaches available today. It has provided valuable insights into the role of the unconscious mind and the importance of early experiences in shaping an individual's psychological well-being. However, it's worth noting that contemporary psychotherapy encompasses a wide range of therapeutic modalities, each with its unique principles and techniques. As a young teacher of mental disorders and psychotherapy, you have the opportunity to explore and share a variety of therapeutic perspectives with your students, allowing them to develop a well-rounded understanding of the field.

This example illustrates the profound impact of early life experiences on an individual's emotional well-being and life patterns. It's a tragic story of how unresolved childhood issues can persist and influence one's adult life, ultimately leading to devastating consequences. Your proposed steps for addressing such cases reflect the principles of psychodynamic therapy and the importance of uncovering and healing these deep-seated wounds. Let's break down these steps

Step 1: Free Association for Catharsis and Self-Awareness

Using the technique of free association, the client is encouraged to express thoughts and emotions freely, without censorship. This process helps the client access repressed or unconscious feelings, leading to emotional release (catharsis). It also fosters self-awareness by allowing the client to explore their patterns of emotions, thoughts, and beliefs.

Step 2: Identifying Unfinished Business

This step involves identifying and addressing the "unfinished business" from childhood, including unmet desires, needs, and past experiences. Understanding and acknowledging these unresolved issues is a critical aspect of psychodynamic therapy.

Step 3: Creating New Life Narrative

Clients are guided to construct new life narratives that incorporate a reevaluation of the past, present, and future. This process aims to reframe the client's perspective and foster personal growth and healing.

Step 4: Integrating Personal Narratives into Family and Social Contexts

The final step involves exploring and integrating the revised personal narratives within the context of family and social relationships. This step emphasizes how changes in one's understanding and perspective can impact their interactions with others.

These steps reflect a therapeutic process that encourages individuals to confront and heal the emotional wounds from their past. By doing so, clients can develop a deeper self-awareness, revise their life narratives, and ultimately improve their emotional well-being and relationships. The tragic example shared serves as a poignant reminder of the significance of addressing these deep-seated emotional issues through therapy to prevent further suffering.

Psychodynamic family therapy is an approach to family therapy that integrates the fundamental concepts of psychoanalytical theory, emphasizing the necessity of addressing the unconscious aspects of an individual's functioning, as well as their development within a social context, particularly within the family unit. Adult patterns of emotions, beliefs, and thoughts often stem from experiences that are suppressed in the depths of the unconscious mind. It is essential to work with each individual within the family to effectively address the family's dynamics within our society.

Psychodynamic family therapy typically involves long-term treatment and is frequently employed in response to chronic family issues, rather than specific, isolated problems. Following the core principles of psychoanalytic therapy, this approach concentrates on exploring the unconscious processes that result from unresolved conflicts within the family unit. These conflicts are analysed from a family perspective.

Therapists guide the family in exploring their family history, examining painful or traumatic experiences, and addressing other issues that have affected family members. By doing so, they work toward resolving long-standing problems within the family. Psychodynamic family therapy plays a pivotal role in identifying deep-rooted issues and fostering a path towards a healthier and happier family life.

Psychodynamic family therapists should be well-versed in several key concepts, including "free association," "catharsis," "Freudian slip," "dream analysis," and various levels of consciousness. These concepts are employed to process the information gathered during family therapy sessions.

Psychodrama is another therapeutic technique often used in group settings. Traditional psychodrama aims to reenact events from an individual's life and typically consists of three key stages.

The session commences with a "warm-up" phase, during which group members start to reflect on specific events from their own lives. Each participant identifies a particular event and subsequently brings it to life through action. These actions are observed by other group members.

In the third part, other group members share how their own stories relate to or mirror the experiences of the individual whose event was enacted. The psychotherapist plays a crucial role in facilitating the process. They may act as the director of this "psychodramatic movie," guiding the protagonist and encouraging various techniques, such as role-reversal, soliloquy, or the use of an empty chair. These techniques are employed to help the individual achieve a profound catharsis, a moment of emotional release and insight.

The goal is to provide a unique and therapeutic experience for the individual, with the end result being a sense of complete relaxation and emotional relief after the cathartic process.

Multigenerational Family therapy

Murray Bowen conducted groundbreaking research on the symbiotic relationship between mothers and their schizophrenic children while working at the Menninger Clinic in Topeka, Kansas. Through his research, he developed the concepts of anxious and functional attachment to characterize the interactional patterns within the mother-child relationship.

In 1954, Bowen was appointed as the inaugural director of the family division at the National Institute of Mental Health (NIMH). Initially, his approach involved providing separate therapists for each individual member of a family. However, he soon realized that this method tended to fragment families rather than foster cohesion among family members. Consequently, he envisioned a new approach that treated the family as a single, interconnected unit, which ultimately led to his significant contributions to the field of family therapy. Bowen became one of the founders of this transformative approach, which focused on addressing issues within the family as a whole rather than in isolation

Murray Bowen's theory of family therapy, often referred to as transgenerational or intergenerational family therapy, is centered around the idea that there are predictable patterns of interpersonal relationships that extend across three generations within a family. These patterns can have a significant impact on the family's dynamics and functioning.

Bowen's theory comprises eight key concepts, each of which plays a crucial role in understanding and addressing family dynamics. These concepts include:

1. Differentiation of self
2. Triangulation
3. The nuclear-family emotional system
4. The family projection process
5. The multigenerational transmission processes
6. Sibling position
7. Emotional cutoff
8. Societal regression

These concepts are integral to Bowen's approach and provide valuable insights into the dynamics of family relationships. They are often explored in depth within academic circles and family therapy training to help therapists and professionals better understand and work with families.

Emotional triangles are fundamental components of family systems theory. These triangles represent a three-person relationship system, which is considered the smallest and most stable form of relationship within a family.

An emotional triangle is a relationship dynamic involving three individuals. It is the smallest and most stable unit within a family system. Two-person relationships can often become strained when confronted with difficulties, but the addition of a third person in the family can help distribute and alleviate tensions. This third person can act as a mediator and provide support to the couple, especially when it comes to dealing with stressors.

However, if a triangle is unable to effectively manage the tensions within it, it can lead to the formation of additional triangles involving other family members. While these new triangles may temporarily help distribute the stress, there is often less potential for resolving the underlying problems experienced by the individual or the family as a whole.

Differentiation of Self: is a core concept in family systems theory, primarily developed by Murray Bowen. It pertains to an individual's ability to separate their own identity and self-esteem from the opinions, judgments, and emotions of others. Here's an improved explanation:

The foundation of an individual's sense of self is influenced by their genetic makeup, but early life experiences, particularly during childhood and adolescence, play a significant role in the development of one's self-identity. This process of self-development is continuous and evolves throughout a person's life. People who struggle with differentiation of self often rely on external validation and approval from others to feel complete. They shape their thoughts, words, and actions in a way that they believe will impress others, in the hope of gaining acceptance and approval.

Bowen describes a three-step process that an individual goes through in their effort to define themselves:

1. **Reacting**: In response to external factors, individuals may react emotionally, often seeking validation or attempting to please others.
2. **Voicing disapproval**: As individuals become more aware of their own needs and values, they may express disapproval when their preferences or beliefs clash with those of others.
3. **Demanding the other to change back**: This stage involves a more assertive expression of one's needs and a demand for others to respect their individuality.

To illustrate, consider a marital relationship. In a two-person relationship, such as that between a husband and wife, there is often a sense of equilibrium. They share attention, love, and care with each other. However, when a third person, such as a child, enters the family, this equilibrium can be disrupted. The introduction of a third member into the family unit can lead to a shift in roles and dynamics.

In such situations, the three steps of asserting one's self may come into play, particularly from the person who feels like an "outsider" in the new family triangle. This process can be complex and may involve efforts to regain a sense of self and identity within the changed family dynamic.

Nuclear Family Systems

Murray Bowen's family systems theory provides insights into how families deal with anxiety. According to Bowen, there are three main mechanisms through which the family system copes with anxiety:

1. **Family Conflict:** Family conflict can serve as a way to manage anxiety. When tensions arise within the family, they can be a means of diverting focus from the underlying anxieties to more immediate issues or disagreements. These conflicts might create a temporary distraction from the anxiety but don't necessarily resolve the core issues.
2. **Physical, Social, and Psychological Illness:** Bowen also observed that in some cases, family members might develop physical, social, or psychological illnesses as a way of dealing with anxiety. These issues can draw attention away from underlying family tensions and be a manifestation of the anxiety within the family system.

Bowen's theory emphasizes that managing anxiety in the family system is often a complex and dynamic process. He also highlights the importance of differentiation of self, which allows family members to manage their anxiety in a more adaptive and constructive way. Instead of resorting to these mechanisms, individuals with higher self-differentiation are better able to maintain their individuality while still being emotionally connected to the family system, thus reducing the need for these coping mechanisms.

Family Projective Process

Projection is another mechanism whereby individuals in the family attribute their own anxieties and problems to others. By projecting their issues onto someone else, they can temporarily relieve themselves of the burden of dealing with their anxieties directly. This can lead to scapegoating or blaming, where one family member becomes the target for projecting anxieties and issues.

Multi-generational transmission process

This concept refers to the transfer of the ability to foster healthy and intimate relationships within a family from one generation to the next. A skilled therapist identifies patterns that persist, whether they are positive or negative, and works to reinforce positive patterns that enhance family well-being while addressing and reducing negative patterns that contribute to distress and anxiety in relationships. The family therapist also places importance on normalizing challenges by helping clients understand that conflicts and tensions can persist even after the therapy sessions have ended.

Example

Generation 1: This generation strictly adhered to patriarchal norms. The grandfather, as the head of the joint family, held sole decision-making authority. Other family members, though often dissatisfied with these decisions, had little room to voice their objections. Obedience and contributing to the family's well-being were expected, especially from female members who were primarily homemakers with no opportunity for outside employment.

Generation 2: The second generation sought to shift towards nuclear families, aiming to redistribute authority and gain more autonomy in decision-making. However, the enduring influence of past interaction patterns, self-concepts, and rigid adherence to established rules and norms led to heightened stress and anxiety in their family dynamics, perpetuating these patterns.

Present Generation: The current generation views these patterns through a new socio-cultural lens. Employing a Bowenian approach, they identify and address the negative patterns, creating a fresh framework for developing healthier, more intimate family relationships.

Emotional cutoff

Frequently, individuals harbor unresolved issues within their original families, particularly with their siblings. These unresolved matters often give rise to tension and anxiety, leading some clients to cope by distancing themselves from their original family. Unresolved attachment issues can manifest in various ways.

Example

Ms. Abhi has relocated to Australia, living far from her parents in India. Unresolved emotional attachments from her early years continue to trigger severe anxiety. Pressure from her parents to conform to their expectations resulted in a decision to distance herself from the family. Despite the physical separation, she maintains regular contact with her parents and occasionally makes painful visits, often feeling apprehensive about the outcomes. The therapist's role is to inquire whether cutting off from the family due to unresolved emotional issues has a positive effect or if these issues resurface in other relationships. Cutting off from unresolved emotional issues can serve as a coping mechanism, but the therapist's aim is to empower the client to resolve these emotional challenges.

Sibling Position

Sibling position can indeed play a role in shaping personality and characteristics. Bowen's family research has identified common characteristics associated with individuals occupying the same sibling positions. For instance, the oldest sibling often takes on leadership roles, while the youngest sibling tends to follow. These positions can influence future relationships and family dynamics. It's important to analyze and understand these common characteristics within different sibling positions, as exploring them in the context of family therapy can reveal patterns that may negatively impact personal development and family interactions. This understanding can be valuable in addressing and resolving issues within the family.

Sibling rivalry can indeed be influenced by the unique characteristics associated with each sibling's position within the family, as well as how these characteristics are validated or rejected by the parents. It's not uncommon for clients to feel invalidated or incapable when compared to their siblings, which can impact their self-esteem and self-perception.

In therapy, it's crucial for the therapist to explore these deep-rooted experiences and emotions. Validating the client's feelings and the need to rework their self-concept, including the characteristics associated with their sibling position, is a valuable step. The therapist can work with the client to develop new, practical characteristics that empower them and help them build a healthier self-identity outside of their sibling position, ultimately fostering improved self-esteem and personal growth.

Societal Emotional Process

The emotional system that operates at a societal level has a profound impact on shaping behaviors and can lead to both progressive and regressive periods within society. This system encompasses key elements, including the differentiation of self, emotional triangles, and the dynamics within the nuclear family emotional system. This emotional system is a driving force that can either foster societal progress or lead to regressive periods, depending on how these components interact and influence human behavior.

Other concepts of Bowenian Therapy

In the context of family systems theory, **anxiety,** as defined by Murray Bowen, represents emotional tension experienced by family members. According to Bowen, this anxiety often originates from within the family system itself. The central objective in comprehending and addressing this anxiety is to alleviate the emotional tension experienced by family members. A common coping mechanism employed by individuals within a family system to mitigate this anxiety is triangulation, a process that involves introducing another person or element into the family dynamic to help release emotional tension.

Over time, as family members continually resort to triangulation as a means of managing anxiety, it can disrupt the equilibrium of the couple's relationship. This disruption may lead to an ongoing need for triangulation as emotional tension increases, perpetuating a cycle of dependence on external factors to manage the family's emotional dynamics.

Bowen's family systems theory places significant emphasis on differentiation over fusion in family dynamics. Fusion, as defined by Bowen, describes a state where individuals become emotionally entangled or excessively reliant on each other, often resulting in various challenges. In contrast, **differentiation** is a process wherein individuals maintain a strong sense of self while still fostering emotional connections with others. Highly differentiated individuals have the capacity to remain composed and steady even when confronted with emotional turmoil, making them instrumental in reducing anxiety within the family.

Bowen's work highlights the critical importance of striking a balance between togetherness and separateness within family systems. Overly fused relationships tend to exacerbate anxiety and dysfunction, while emphasizing differentiation can contribute to more robust and harmonious family dynamics. This underscores the significance of individuality and self-regulation within the context of healthy familial relationships.

Bowen emphasized the family therapy should help in reducing anxiety and finding the symptoms experienced by the members. The symptoms could be relived trough a process of differentiation of self, such as thinking v/s feeling. Murray Bowen's family therapy approach includes several techniques, two of which are significant in understanding and working with family dynamics:

Genogram: A genogram is a comprehensive visual representation of a family's structure and history. It surpasses the simplicity of a family tree by not only encompassing births, deaths, and relationships but also significant life events, recurring patterns, and issues across multiple generations. The primary objective of creating a genogram is to provide a clear visual and analytical insight into the family's dynamics and relationships. Each symbol and line within a genogram holds vital information regarding family members, their roles, and their interconnections. For instance, diverse types of lines may be used to denote various relationships or connections, including conflicts. Within the context of therapy, the "index person" (IP) is the family member under scrutiny, and the genogram aids in comprehending their position within the family structure and any patterns they might be replicating from previous generations.

Asking Questions: Bowen's therapeutic approach places significant emphasis on the art of asking pertinent questions. These questions are designed to delve into the client's familial role, their inner psychological dynamics, and their level of self-differentiation. The intent behind these inquiries is to acquire a deeper understanding of how the client contributes to familial conflicts, how they align with family patterns, and the manner in which they approach and react to familial issues. This information proves invaluable for family therapists in evaluating the root causes of familial challenges and guiding clients in comprehending their roles and relationships within the family system. Effective questioning stands as a cornerstone skill in family therapy, fostering self-reflection and insight in the client and ultimately enhancing their interactions with other family members.

Both genograms and effective questioning are essential tools and techniques in Bowen's family therapy approach, helping therapists and families gain a deeper understanding of the family system and how it impacts individual members. These methods contribute to the process of differentiation and healthier family dynamics.

Structural Family Therapy (SFT)

Salvador Minuchin is recognized as a champion of Structural Family Therapy (SFT). In his work with children, he identified concerning behavior patterns that required intervention. To address these issues, he involved not just the child but also their parents, siblings, and extended family as sources of support and encouragement. This comprehensive approach proved to be more effective than individual support, as it leveraged the family as a unified unit to modify behaviors and reduce negative emotions and thoughts.

Structural Family Therapy places significant importance on the family's structure. It focuses on roles, boundaries, hierarchy, and subsystems within the family. Minuchin's groundbreaking interventions were backed by evidence-based research.

One key concept in Structural Therapy is "boundaries." Boundaries are the rules that govern the physical and psychological distances between family members. These boundaries are often influenced by the family's cultural context. Some individuals may require more personal space than others, and family members are encouraged to respect these individual needs.

An example of this was demonstrated during a premarital counselling session. A couple was given ropes to draw boundaries around themselves. One partner drew a small circle, expressing a desire for close physical and psychological proximity, while the other drew a larger circle, signifying a need for more private space. This exercise highlighted the importance of open communication and negotiation between family members to address boundary issues and foster healthy relationships.

Salvador Minuchin's Structural Family Therapy (SFT) encompasses several key concepts related to family boundaries, roles, and therapeutic phases. Here's a breakdown of these components:

Family Boundaries:

1. **Clear Boundaries**: In families with clear boundaries, there's close emotional contact while allowing each family member to maintain a sense of individual identity.
2. **Enmeshment and Diffuse Boundaries**: In this scenario, individual autonomy is jeopardized. Family members may take credit for each other's achievements and blur the lines of individual identity, erasing boundaries.
3. **Rigid Boundaries**: Families with rigid boundaries focus on individual autonomy, often to the detriment of relational issues. These boundaries are inflexible and resistant to reorganization, which can cause marital problems.

Therapeutic Emphasis:

- SFT emphasizes the family as a whole rather than addressing individual issues first. The goal is to identify and modify negative habits and behaviors that contribute to conflicts, transforming them into healthier and more positive ones to foster family stability and love.

Enactments:

- Enactments involve re-enacting conflicts within the family, allowing the therapist to observe and modify the family structure. It helps the family explore different communication and interaction options, ultimately creating clearer and more engaging boundaries and improving roles and relationships.

Sub-systems:

- Sub-systems are created within the family as needed. For instance, if a couple needs to work on relationship-engaging boundaries, a sub-system may be established between the spouses, excluding the children. The therapist works on changing boundaries, and the children are later brought in to check the effects of the new boundaries on the family.

Phases of Therapy: Minuchin's SFT comprises three stages:

1. **Building Alliance**: The therapist accommodates the family's style and language, observing their structure, hierarchies, and cultural influences.
2. **Assessment**: The therapist evaluates the family structure, boundaries, and hierarchical control.
3. **Addressing Issues**: Active transformation of the family structure is undertaken to reduce symptoms causing discord.

Steps within Therapy:

1. Identify family structure, roles, habits, and boundaries.
2. Identify specific issues to address holistically.
3. Explore family dynamics causing tension, preparing a treatment plan.
4. Provide a space for family members to express themselves, sometimes by escalating situations to facilitate ventilation.
5. Promote positive family dynamics to create a healthier family overall.

Minuchin's SFT emphasizes the importance of understanding family structure, boundaries, and hierarchies to address issues and create a more harmonious family environment.

Human Validation Process Model

Virginia Satir was indeed a prominent figure in the field of family therapy, and her approach focused on promoting healthy family dynamics through open and reciprocal sharing of affection, feelings, and love. Here's a brief overview of some of her key concepts and techniques:

1. **Healthy Family Life:** Satir emphasized the importance of open and reciprocal sharing of affection, feelings, and love in a healthy family. She believed that fostering genuine emotional expression within the family was vital for positive relationships.

2. **Family Roles:** Satir introduced various family roles, such as "the rescuer" and "the placator," which were descriptions of common roles individuals might take on within a family. These roles could influence and sometimes constrain family interactions and relationships.

3. **Counselor-Family Rapport:** Satir stressed the significance of building a strong rapport between the family and the counselor. A strong therapeutic relationship is often seen as the foundation for effective family therapy.

4. **Validation of Self-Esteem:** Satir placed importance on validating the self-esteem of family members. Recognizing and respecting each family member's self-worth and self-esteem is a central aspect of her approach.

5. **Family Rules:** Satir explored the unspoken and unwritten rules within families that could impact family dynamics. Understanding and challenging these rules, when necessary, was part of her therapeutic process.

6. **Communication Patterns:** Satir delved into communication patterns within the family, including both verbal and non-verbal communication. She sought to identify and address dysfunctional communication habits that might hinder effective family interaction.

7. **Sculpting:** Satir introduced the technique of sculpting, where family members physically position themselves to represent their emotional positions or relationships within the family. This technique helped make underlying emotions and dynamics visible.

8. **Nurturing Triads:** Satir used the concept of nurturing triads to understand the ways family members related to one another. These triads could reveal patterns of closeness or distance within the family.

9. **Family Mapping:** Creating a family map, often through the use of genograms, allowed for a visual representation of the family's structure and history.

10. **Family Life-Fact Chronologies:** Documenting significant events and experiences in the family's history, known as family life-fact chronologies, could provide insight into the family's development and functioning.

Virginia Satir's approach to family therapy emphasizes the importance of understanding and addressing family dynamics, communication, and emotional expression to foster healthier and more functional family relationships. Her work has had a lasting impact on the field of family therapy.

Goals of Human Validation Process Model

Virginia Satir's family therapy approach is rooted in the goal of promoting open and healthy communication within the family. This approach encourages every family member to express themselves honestly, sharing their perceptions, emotions, thoughts, and feelings without the fear of judgment. It places emphasis on exploring both individual and family needs, recognizing the uniqueness of each family member while also considering the collective needs of the family as a whole.

Differences and conflicts within the family are not avoided but rather embraced as opportunities for growth. The counselor facilitates the exploration of these differences and conflicts to enhance family development. Various techniques, including **family sculpting, family reconstruction, and parts parties**, are employed to create awareness within the family. These techniques help family members understand their roles, relationships, and the impact of past experiences. This, in turn, fosters improved communication, self-awareness, and overall family well-being. Satir's approach focuses on strengthening family bonds and enhancing the emotional health of all its members.

Innovations in family therapy

Post-modernists introduced the concept that a healthy family can be constructed through the power of interaction, a perspective often referred to as 'social constructionism.' In this view, a family that engages in positive, healthy, and supportive interactions is more likely to lead a happy and meaningful family life. Therefore, therapists in this approach focus on enhancing these interactions, encompassing both verbal and non-verbal as well as symbolic forms of communication. The role of the therapist is to facilitate and improve these interactions, fostering a stronger and more satisfying family dynamic.

"The Reflective Team"- Tom Andersen

Andersen, a prominent figure in systemic family therapy, introduced the 'Reflecting Team' approach in Norway. In this innovative therapy method, the therapists conduct an interview with a family in one room, while a team of consulting psychologists observes the session from behind a two-way mirror in another room. The psychologists closely observe the interaction and dialogue within the family, paying particular attention to the stories and various narrative elements being shared. The goal is to identify and reflect upon the existing narratives and, in some cases, to seek alternative narratives that can lead to positive change within the family system. This approach offers a unique and valuable perspective on family dynamics and communication, ultimately contributing to the therapeutic process.

Narrative Approach: Michael White and David Epston

This approach focuses on gaining a deep understanding of personal experiences and emphasizes the distinction between being 'childish' and 'childlike' in one's perception of reality. While someone might prefer to be seen as 'childlike,' they may not appreciate being labeled as 'childish.' The critical aspect here is to encourage clients to deconstruct unproductive narratives and construct or reauthor new, productive ones. The therapist plays a crucial role in externalizing the client's problems, effectively separating them from the client. This shift in perspective allows the client to examine the problem from a systemic viewpoint.

Several techniques are employed in this process:

1. **Externalizing:** This technique distinguishes the person from the problem, considering the problems as separate entities from the individual.
2. **Determining Responsibility:** The therapist challenges the client to consider who is in charge, whether it's the person or the problem itself.
3. **Reauthoring the Whole Story:** The therapist encourages the client to reconstruct their narrative, infusing it with more productive elements.
4. **Reinforcing the New Story:** The client works on reconstructing productive and healthy narratives to replace the old, unhelpful ones. This process aims to empower the client with more constructive stories and perspectives.

CHAPTER IV

PARENTING: STYLES, SKILLS, FAULTS AND IMPACTS

Children raised without positive parenting may face numerous issues, including low self-esteem, challenges in forming committed relationships, problematic interaction patterns, ineffective communication skills, and the potential for psychopathology later in life. Modern family members need to learn and identify effective parenting styles and skills to ensure the holistic well-being of future generations. Research studies have shown that faulty parenting can have far-reaching effects not only on children but on future generations as well.

There is no one-size-fits-all parenting style, as each parent may need to adapt their approach depending on the situation. Questions like 'Am I a good parent?' and 'Have I failed as a parent?' often trouble today's parents. During counselling sessions, parents frequently express guilt regarding their children's behavior, friendships, habits, and even addiction. They may blame themselves or point fingers at their spouses, attributing the failure of skillful parenting and child-rearing. In reality, all parents have their limitations, shortcomings, and limited knowledge. They raise their families as they see fit, but sometimes they neglect to listen and adjust their parenting styles or correct their mistakes.

The play 'Two Fathers' explores the roles of fathers in their children's lives. In this play, M.K. Gandhi and the renowned scientist Albert Einstein reflect on their relationships with their respective son and daughter. Gandhi's eldest son left the Ashram, married outside, and even attended his father's funeral from afar, as he was not allowed to be there, eventually passing away. Albert Einstein, on the other hand, disowned his daughter, who was suffering from psychosis. These two great figures had their reasons, and their children had their own issues. However, the play delves into a retrospective conversation where they question if they could have done things differently with their children. This emotional exchange between parents and children reveals a desire for alternative approaches but often a reluctance to consider reworking their parenting styles, skills, and mistakes. If even these stalwarts had challenges in their parenting, it underscores that others can as well.

Parents must identify their parenting styles, skills, and failures and collaborate with family therapists to enhance their relationships with their children. Passing down effective parenting styles from one generation to the next is crucial for promoting psychological and relational well-being. Failing to do so can significantly impact a child's early psychological development and lead to lifelong neurosis. Let's explore different parenting styles with some examples.

a. Authoritative Parenting or Lion Parenting

Have you ever tried discussing matters with a lion? Success is unlikely because this is akin to an authoritative parenting style. In this style, there is little room for negotiation or discussion. The parent's commands are to be followed without question, with communication often being one-way – the others are expected to listen, accept, and obey. Punishments may be common for non-compliance, and nurturing is limited. Flexibility for other family members is often lacking.

For instance, one family had a father with a highly authoritative parenting style. The wife and two daughters were expected to conform to his 'my way or the highway' attitude. This approach led to continuous conflicts within the family, even though they were well-educated and financially stable. The father's mood swings disrupted peace at home, resulting in frequent outbursts of anger, turning evenings into chaotic times. The daughters often consoled their mother, and they sought external assistance to rebuild family relationships, involving third parties and more. They even contemplated escaping family life, but fears held them back.

The lasting scars on children due to faulty parenting styles are a serious concern that should be studied by modern researchers. Premarital counselling should emphasize parenting styles and their significant impact on future generations.

The daughters in this family grew up with a strong aversion to marriage and family life due to the pervasive family discord and the authoritative parenting style. As a result, they continue to struggle when it comes to establishing long-term marital relationships.

This family's interaction pattern, characterized by daily family conflicts and authoritarian parenting, has left a profound impact on the daughters. It has shaped their perceptions and attitudes towards marriage and family, making it challenging for them to engage in stable, long-lasting relationships. The constant exposure to discord and the absence of open communication may have influenced their view of family life as a source of stress and conflict, leading to their reluctance to embrace it in their own lives.

Analysis

The father in this family inherited his parenting style from his own father, and on the surface, the logic may seem sound. However, the repercussions of this parenting approach have been far-reaching. His own childhood was situated in a rural setting during a time when the patriarch of the family had the final say. Their exposure to the world beyond their village was minimal.

As the years passed, he transitioned to a metropolitan city, provided an education for his daughters in an urban environment, and aspired to embrace a more modern family lifestyle. However, he clung to his authoritative parenting style and maintained interaction patterns characteristic of an abusive husband.

His parenting approach was shaped by observational learning from his own upbringing and a firm belief that parents could do no wrong. This unwavering belief led him to maintain an authoritarian parenting style, even when it was evident that it contributed to the ongoing conflicts within the family.

Problems faced by children due to this parenting Approach

- Self-esteem issues
- Hostility or aggressiveness
- Constant anger towards parents even after becoming adults
- To avoid punishment, the children could turn out to be liars
- Lack of tolerance could lead to obsessive as well type A personality demonstrating high level of impatience, high competitiveness and even getting tensed easily.
- List of rules: Rules are broken, punishment is the consequence.

b. Laissez faire parenting or Chameleon parenting

"The term 'Laissez-faire' is of French origin and denotes a parenting style characterized by minimal restrictions and rules. In this approach, parents are present but take on the role of friends rather than authority figures. Some species of chameleons, interestingly, do not provide care for their young after hatching, leaving them to fend for themselves. While human parents practicing laissez-faire parenting do not completely alienate themselves from their children, they grant them a sense of total freedom.

Laissez-faire parenting typically arises from a fear of upsetting the child and an inability to say 'No' to their demands. The child's needs and desires take precedence over the parents' own. Specific directives, such as eating habits, playtime, or study schedules, are not imposed on the child. Instead, the child is given autonomy to make these decisions independently, with parents being warm and nurturing but having no expectations from the child.

An example and analysis can help shed further light on this parenting style. The young man was 20 years old and attending college. Unfortunately, he was grappling with addiction issues, involving alcohol, drugs, and self-harm, which had become distressingly common. His most recent demand was for a high-priced bike, costing 2.5 lakhs in Indian rupees. The family, belonging to the middle class, recognized their financial limitations and were prepared to buy a more affordable two-wheeler. However, the young man vehemently refused and resorted to self-harm by slashing his wrists repeatedly in front of his parents. This alarming incident led to his admission for treatment and counseling.

The parents, in hindsight, realized that they had consistently granted their son's every wish. As the only child, they had a strong desire to avoid upsetting him. Their household had become one where there were seemingly no rules. The father often referred to himself as a 'cool dad' and provided his son with financial support, even for alcohol and outings with friends. Regrettably, the boy's addiction issues and severe psychiatric conditions now required urgent attention.

Analysis

The parenting style in this scenario appears to be a permissive or indulgent parenting style, with the father being referred to as a "cool dad" who grants the child's wishes and provides financial support, even for potentially harmful behaviors like alcohol and outings with friends.

The "cool dad" approach, while well-intentioned, can sometimes lead to problems if it lacks appropriate boundaries and guidance. Permissive parenting can result in a lack of structure and discipline for the child, potentially contributing to issues like addiction and self-harm.

As a counselor, your decision not to blame the parents but to focus on understanding and helping them is a compassionate and effective approach. Blaming parents, especially in situations like these, may not be productive in the counselling process. Instead, it's often more helpful to work collaboratively with the family to address the underlying issues, promote healthier interaction patterns, and provide the necessary support for the young man's deaddiction treatment and recovery.

Problems faced by children due to this parenting Approach

- Problem in Academics
- Behavioral problems (the child has not been reprimanded)
- Lack of acceptance of authority and leadership
- Low self-esteem issues
- Obesity
- Dental problems (it is strange) but the child was not forced in the initial stage to take brushing seriously has its effects.

c. **Intrusive parenting or chicken parenting**

Erik Erikson's theory of psychosocial development indeed emphasizes the stage of autonomy in early childhood, where children are encouraged to explore, make choices, and develop a sense of independence and confidence. This is a critical stage in fostering a child's individuality and self-esteem.

In contrast, the parenting style you mention, characterized by over-pampering and over-intrusiveness, can hinder a child's development of autonomy. When parents do everything for their child and constantly express doubt in the child's ability to handle tasks independently, it can create a sense of dependence and undermine the child's self-confidence.

It's important for parents to strike a balance between providing support and allowing their children to take age-appropriate risks and make their own choices. This balance helps children develop the skills and confidence necessary for healthy autonomy and individuality. Understanding and applying age-appropriate guidance and support is crucial for fostering a child's healthy development.

It's interesting to see how a phone counselling session highlighted the impact of intrusive parenting on a young adult. The scenario you describe illustrates the potential consequences of overprotective or intrusive parenting, where the child's independence and autonomy are stifled.

In this case, the client's desire to get married and move out of the family home to experience independence is a clear indication of the need for autonomy and individuality. It's crucial for parents to recognize that fostering independence and autonomy is a fundamental aspect of healthy child development, especially as children transition into adulthood.

Your initial intuition to assess for dependent personality disorder was insightful, and it's essential to consider the influence of parenting styles in clinical assessments. Addressing these dynamics and helping both the parent and the young adult understand and work through them can be a valuable aspect of counselling and therapy. It can promote personal growth and healthier relationships within the family.

Analysis

The parenting approach described, which involves constant interference and overprotectiveness, can indeed have negative consequences for the child's development. Here are some key points to consider:

1. **Lack of Individuality:** Constant interference can stifle a child's ability to develop their own identity and make independent choices. This can lead to a lack of individuality, where the child may struggle to assert themselves or make decisions in the future.

2. **Detestation of Help:** Over time, the child may grow to resent or detest individuals who constantly come to their aid, as they may associate such help with an inability to do things on their own. This can impact their relationships and social interactions.

3. **Self-Esteem and Mental Health:** Intrusive parenting can harm a child's self-esteem and self-confidence. It may lead to feelings of inadequacy and self-doubt, which can contribute to behavioral and mental health issues in the future.

4. **Need for Positive Change:** It's essential for parents to recognize the potential harm of this parenting style and be willing to evaluate and modify their approach. Acknowledging past mistakes and implementing a new, more balanced approach to parenting is crucial for better child rearing and overall family well-being.

Parenting should aim to strike a balance between providing guidance, support, and protection while allowing children to explore and develop their own capabilities. Encouraging autonomy and independence within age-appropriate boundaries is essential for healthy child development.

Problems faced by children due to this parenting Approach

- Self-esteem issues
- Behavioral and emotional problems
- Dependence
- Inability to understand self-worth and a sense of achievement.
- Anger towards the parents or the authority.

d. Teddy Bear Parenting

Attachment parenting emphasizes the importance of nurturing and maintaining close physical proximity with the child's primary caregiver, typically the mother or father. The attachment theory, initially developed by John Bowlby, underscores the significance of a secure attachment between the child and the caregiver during the early stages of development.

Key points from your explanation:

1. **Child's Needs and Communication:** Attachment parenting recognizes a child's cries as a form of communication rather than manipulation. It acknowledges that a child cries to express their needs, and responding to those needs is vital for building a secure attachment.

2. **Constant Care and Physical Proximity:** Attachment parenting involves the primary caregiver being consistently close to the child, providing skin-to-skin contact, and responding to the child's cries at any time of the day. This high level of responsiveness is believed to foster a secure attachment.

3. **Parental Sacrifice:** Practicing attachment parenting often requires the primary caregiver to prioritize the child's needs and well-being over their own. This self-sacrifice can lead to fatigue and weariness for the caregiver.

4. **Transition to Autonomy:** Attachment parenting is typically more prominent in the early stages of a child's life. As the child grows and becomes more autonomous, some aspects of attachment parenting may naturally evolve.

Attachment parenting is associated with fostering a strong parent-child bond and a sense of security in the child. However, this style may gradually shift as the child develops more independence. It's important for parents to adapt their parenting approach to meet the changing needs of their child as they grow and develop.

Problems faced by children due to this parenting Approach

- Behavioral issues
- Need for physical proximity in relationship

CHAPTER V

MARITAL DISCORDS AND ITS EFFECT ON THE CHILDREN

The dictionary meaning of the word discord is, "The <u>state</u> of not <u>agreeing</u> or <u>sharing</u> <u>opinions</u> or lack of trust between people. (Cambridge). There is a famous saying of the olden days that goes as, "Marriages are made in heaven"; these principles need to be changed as, Marriages are built on trust in the present era. Ed Tronick and Claudia M. Gold in their book called power of Discord argue that discord in relationships bound to come; and it ought to be solved by the trust that the relationship is able to hold on with each other. Any relationship demands fraternal understanding and filial trust. When that point fades away, challenges bump in, making the life harder and tougher. This doesn't affect only the twosomes but links to the negative impact of the children that includes academic, emotional and social behaviour.

Marital discord can destructively influence the children by crafting a nerve-wracking environment. Endless arguments, aggression or a lack of emotive support can lead to unhinged emotional and social relationships. (Grych & Fincham, 2001) Children may suffer academically, declining in their performance, exhibit aggression in their relationships or experience anxiety and depression that cannot be expressive easily. In the long term these effects may include difficulties in forming healthy relationships as adults and framing their own families and a higher likelihood of experiencing sound mental health. It underlines the importance of maintaining a healthy and supportive family environment for the well-being.

Chronic discord between parents is a risk factor for a variety of child problems, including poor emotional adjustment, low self-esteem, aggression in peer relationships, and delinquency (Davies & Cummings, 1994; Emery, 1999).

CHARACTERISTICS OF CHILDREN FROM CONJUGAL BLISSFUL FAMILIES

There was a research conducted in a small classroom of 30 students, using the observation method. The class was given a task to complete within a given period of time. Astonishingly, 6 children topped all the other extraordinarily. Once the task was completed, the background of the students was studied carefully. The research revealed that the children who were able to successfully complete the task had a very good parental support and upbringing. They had very strong reasoning capacities, emotional support, socio –economic, psychological and spiritual well-being. Based on the above conducted research, the following characteristics are drawn.

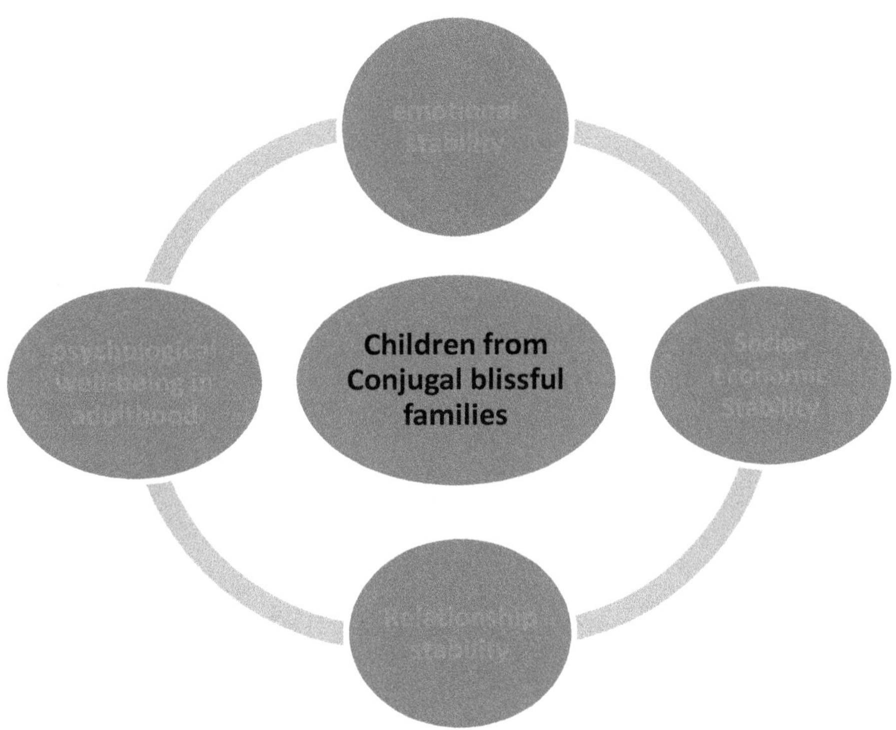

1. Emotional Stability:

Emotional stability is the ability to maintain a composed and reliable emotional state, even in the midst of stressful and challenging situations. It is a capacity to regulate being more flexible and knowing to manage the emotions in a healthy and a constructive way. In other words, it's a matured way of responding to one's emotions.

This art of standing firm or managing the emotions become easy for the children who are brought up by blissful marital families. The children from the background of marital harmony, will be able to withstand any challenging phase of life, to which, misunderstandings, temporary conflicts and fights are not an exemption. The children brought up in such a family learns to cope up the situations from parents. The early stage of childhood teaches the skill of observing and the stage of adulthood the skill of practicing.

Children from Blissful marital families, often display emotional well- being both inside and outside the families. Emotional stability within the family is very essential for a child's healthy and matured growth. Below are few examples that illustrate how this stability aids to a child's well-being.

Inside the family:

a. **Free dialogue:** The children from healthy parenting families grow in open dialogues and express their thoughts, ideas and feeling without fear. They grow positively healthy, with the sense of openness to share and clarify everything to their parents.

Example: The parents encourage children to discuss, make certain choices and express their decisions without any judgemental backgrounds. This free and natural environment allow children to grow in open communication.

b. **Feeling of protection:** The child reliably receives sufficient care, love, attention and affection from the parents. This fosters to a secured feeling that the child is loved by parents and explores a more assertive and confident actions; this in turn enables the child to anchor the emotions in a healthy manner.

Example: When corrected by the parents, the children express a kind of reluctance to accept in the beginning but later understands and clings to parents without parting from them. If a child faces a challenge in handling emotions like fear, anger and sadness, it recourses to parents for assistance.

c. **Emotive Support:** Emotional stability of the parents, lead to emotional support of the children in the family. When parents are emotionally matured, they guide the children in the same manner.

Example: Children brought up by the parents with strong marital bond are equipped to support in the development of a child's emotional flexibility. In the circle of its' friends, if a situation of misunderstanding arises, the child would deal better than the child whose parents do not have a good relationship among themselves.

d. **A disciplined life:** A healthy disciplined life is the first step towards handling emotions in a healthy manner. Every family has their own beliefs and boundaries in which they would want their children to grow. By setting up certain limits, family provides the responsibility and structure for the children develop self-discipline and navigate social situations with respect for others' needs and feelings.

e. **Sense of belonging:** The sense of belongingness is a feeling where a child feels loved and accepted within the family. Many of the problems can find solution in themselves if one knows how to own them and work through them; to which sense of belongingness acts as a good equipment. If a child feels loved and accepted, the child understands others and lives a matured emotional life.

Example: Holding everyday free conversations with the children about their daily schedules and activities and standing by them in their challenges and struggles which make them feel that the parents are a part of their lives.

f. **Role Modelling:** The parents are the best role models for their children. If parents are emotionally balanced, the children learn from them. Children derive their values from the way their parents live. A right way to bring the children to a quality life is to create a place of values for themselves and for others in a sense of mutual acceptance.

Example: Children observe how their parents deal with the problems and how they balance their emotions such as anger, fear and depression and deal with them.

Outside the family:

a. **Peer relationship:** The children from Conjugal Blissful Families will know the values of relationships and grow in fraternal living. They learn to live amicably amidst the varieties of cultures and situations.

Example: The child observes how the parents deal with their relationship issues and in turn reflects the same on the peer group.

b. **Extra -curricular activities:** The children grow very freely and independently and excel in the activities with the positive support of the parents.

Example: The child growing in a joyful atmosphere of the parents become more positive and works towards achieving extra-curricular activities along with the regular activities of the day.

c. **Coping with stress:** The child learns to cope up with the issues of stress easily, as parents create very supportive environment.

Example: Children manage their stress through involvement in games or creatively doing the routine things.

SOCIOECONOMIC ATTAINMENT

Socio- Economic fulfilment denotes to the accomplished grade and realization of persons or individuals within the societal and fiscal structure. Every family in large or small capacity aims for the good socio-economic status. This not only increases the rank in the society, but serves in boosting up one's morale in the society. A major mediator of the link between economic hardship and parenting behaviour is psychological distress deriving from an excess of negative life events, undesirable chronic conditions, and the absence and disruption of marital bonds, (Vonnie C. McLoyd, 1990). The unsettled or disturbed marital bonds may affect not only the life style but the work performance, which in turn results in the economic welfare of the family and interrupts the family well-being. To attain the economic stability, the family bound by the good morale and emotional support becomes a primary requirement.

In addition to this, the communal prospects and customs concerning to marriage can have its effect on the certain social structures and opportunities, further prompting the economic outcomes. On the over all, the stress and strains in marital relationship due to discords and disharmony affects both marital happiness and the socio-economic growth of the individual as a family if the discords sustain to a great extent. The below points from the study supports the statement that the children from blissful marital families enjoy a healthy socio-economic status.

An ability for excellence schooling: The quality of education that one receives is the quality of one's living. The person with good education sustains not only the growth of the individual, but the society. The education trains a person for a good reasonable, analytical and critical thinking. The children with good education become the asset of the nation. This can be achieved only through the excellence schooling that the child receives.

According to the National Achievement Survey 2017 for the grades 3, 5 and 8 only 45.2 per cent of students have achieved the targeted performance levels across all subjects and classes at the national level. Which means to say, the quality or the standard of the quality education is less than half of the targeted population. The reasons for failure for the quality education can vary from one to the other.

The National Library of Medicine 2009, states that the study was performed on a total 699 children who were classified as school failures. Social reasons include living with one parent 26.9%, parental divorce (27%) parents showing no interest in their child's education and school system (41.6%), low income (19.3%), and smoking (19.6%). From the above data, it becomes evident that the social reasons which include parental divorce and disinterest of the parents on the children add on to the decline in the school going students, and eventually this leads to poor socio-economic status of the country.

Physical wellness: Good health is not only the expression of a full normality in the function of the organism, but also stability in the totality of the complex faculty that goes under the name of mind. Work, tension and healthiness are contributed directly to the socio-economic factor. Children of the well-being family experience good health to a great extent. Nutrition, attention on children, health care is very important for physical wellness. If a marital relationship is in discord, this becomes an impossible task for the parents to provide good food to the children. The physical illness in turn offers a defeat to the socio-economic rise up. And hence, physical illness contributes to the downfall of socio-economic status. If marital disputes could be settled between the spouse politely, the further reasons for children's disappointment over food and other health issues do not arise, but in a situation of chronic marital discord, the children suffer lack of attention on food. The health aspect of children could be cornered or ignored by the parents, resulting in the poor health conditions of the children. Any nation without good health cannot see the point of growth, and affects the socio-economic attainment of the country.

Case:1 There was a study conducted among 100 college going adolescents, who were deprived of morning intake of food. The results shown that the children whose parents were in conflicts and were not paying attention to keep the morning food ready were about 19%. And of which girls, being too sensitive shown the highest rate among who do not consume their food due to the marital disputes of the parents.

Hence, the children from conjugal blissful families' experience not only attention and care but overall physical wellness, causing in the good socio-economic status of the nation.

Financial security: Marriage supports the financial security. The satisfied marital or blissful marital life have paved way for many financial securities. Children from such families carry a complete feeling of financial security among themselves. They enjoy a feeling of acceptance and economic safety of their present and future life. Eg: the parents supporting the children worry about the future of the children and invest in different finance securities. This makes the parents feel confident and children too will lead a happy life. In the other hand, children from the families of marital discord struggle to feel the security in themselves, and fail to execute a good socio-economic life.

The survey of few studies display the impact of marital conflict exposure in childhood to a great extent affect the children's physical, emotional, socio-economic and financial security not only in adolescence but carries through their adulthood. There are many chances, that the children witnessing the marital disputes of their parents at the early age can become potential threat to the healthy married life in later stages.

PATTERNS OF PARENT-CHILD RELATIONSHIPS

Child's relationship with parents is of a great significance. The positive experience from the parents encourage the children in good learning and living atmosphere. It encourages the children to bond themselves with the individuals, parents, friends, society and at large the whole universe. A considerable degree of maturity will enhance an eminence life, manifesting a higher cause of living considering the social justice and peace.

As per the observational study conducted the relationship pattern of the parent-child can be divided as follows.

PATTERNS OF PARENT-CHILD RELATIONSHIPS AMONG DISCORD MARRIAGES

i. Isolated pattern of relationship: Isolated pattern refers to the child and parent relationship as I don't bother attitude. In the environment of the parents where there are regular disputes, disagreements and discords, the parents often worry about their own settlements. The mind becomes too restless as to settle the disputes and spares no time for the children. If the children are more than one in number, they might have a sibling to deal with; but in today's pattern of single child in the family, the child often feels isolated from the parents.

Eg: In the olden days there used to be joint families and children share a beautiful bond of many relationships. If parents do not pay attention, there might be many to take care of their needs; which is very crucial comparatively to today's context. The child feels more insecure and abandoned.

The isolated pattern of relationship not only separates child from the bond of parents but also separates themselves from their own identity. The heated arguments and highly unsolvable clashes between the parents irk the child's growth. The isolated pattern of relationship is known to be unhealthy pattern as it doesn't allow the child to grow in the healthy atmosphere. This may lead the child to have negative opinion of the society later in the adult age and hamper the social life of the child.

ii. Too protective pattern of relationship: The parental disputes sometime may lead to the no attention on the child or more attention of the child from either ends. The father or the mother may shift complete focus on the child, not allowing the child to grow independently. One might become too possessive of the child to let go the discord from the spousal end. This pattern can be names as You are my all pattern. Under this, the child sometimes put to the constraint of the parents to oblige and compel itself to remain dependant always, leading to the child's unhealthy social and emotional life. The parents owning the children is appreciative but not possessing as to hinder the natural growth of the child. The child may be unaware of it now and realizes in the later stage.

Eg: The overly protected child feels at one stage of life that it was unable to make decisions on its own; and was very much dependant on her mother/father even for every day's choices regarding the clothing, eating, studies etc.

This kind of pattern of relationship would not allow the children to the growth of maturity, unless the children becoming adults work on their life in later stages.

iii. Dictatorial pattern of relationship: The word dictator according to the oxford dictionary defines itself as, 'a person who behaves as if they have complete power over other people, and tells them what to do'. The dictatorial pattern of relationship deprives one to think and act on their own and induces fear and hatred towards everything. **"No choices, no explanations; no excuses, no apologies"** these might trigger a very negative tone, and this perhaps so. The rule of dictatorship considers nothing of the above. If the parents are too aggressive towards the children and control every aspect without giving them the taste of freedom, choice, dialogue and expression, the child develops an attitude of fear and hatred, which hampers the future growth.

This kind of relationship imposes strict rules on the child and can be called as You are under my control principle. The discords in the marriage life may sometimes lead to the over control of the children.

Eg: The child that is grown under lot of restrictions and conditions without a room for natural love and joy, become passive or active aggressive in later stages. The child if not treated, may learn from its' experience that the world around is very bad and not the place to live.

PATTERNS OF PARENT-CHILD RELATIONSHIPS AMONG BLISSFUL MARRIAGES

i. Friend & Parent pattern of relationship: A child seeks the combination of a parent and a friend relationship in every parent. The parental discipline and guidance in the early childhood blended with a friendly understanding and listening in later stages will make a perfect growth of the children.

It will foster a strong emotional bond and create a safe and supportive environment for the kid to feel comfortable sharing their thoughts and experiences. (Adit Ganguly,2023). It also reassures open and authentic dialogue where the child, who now assesses their folks as their colleague becomes more prone to share their personal feelings. This builds enormous confidence and plays a contributory role in helping the child develop healthy relationships as they grow older.

ii. Credible pattern of relationship: The credible pattern of relationship can be explained as parents being truly loving, understanding, supportive and confident. Only trustworthy parents can generate a contented growth of the children. In order to create good atmosphere to children's creative learning and understanding there should be good communication between the parents and children. Only parents who are free from marital discords and tensions can teach their children to live a stress-free life.

They can communicate with their child easily. Children do not feel like talking to parents who are always under disagreements and disharmony. They do not feel like voicing their thoughts, judgements and glitches to such parents. Hence, it is essential that the parents remain discord free.

iii. **Value based model pattern of relationship:** This particular style of parenthood constructs of itself by the values and quality behaviour of the parents which they wish from their children. The family engage in quality time with each other strengthening their sense of togetherness, sharing lasting memories. They understand the need for discipline with clear boundaries focusing on the growth of each other. The parents give way for respectful interactions, demonstrating empathy and emotional support. This model encourages open communications that create a connective atmosphere of acceptance and evaluation. This way, the relationships become life lasting prized moments.

For children and adolescences, knowing their parents trust them can extend their feeling of protection in the world, boost their self-worth and approval as they try innovative things, and reassure them that they have someone to shelter to when things don't turn up conferring to their plans.

RELATIONSHIP OF A PARENT AND CHILD IN THE EARLY CHILDHOOD TO

Erikson's Psychosocial Stages

Stage	Basic Conflict	Virtue	Description
Infancy 0–1 year	Trust vs. mistrust	Hope	Trust (or mistrust) that basic needs, such as nourishment and affection, will be met
Early childhood 1–3 years	Autonomy vs. shame/doubt	Will	Develop a sense of independence in many tasks
Play age 3–6 years	Initiative vs. guilt	Purpose	Take initiative on some activities—may develop g when unsuccessful or boundaries overstepped
School age 7–11 years	Industry vs. inferiority	Competence	Develop self-confidence in abilities when compet or sense of inferiority when not
Adolescence 12–18 years	Identity vs. confusion	Fidelity	Experiment with and develop identity and roles
Early adulthood 19–29 years	Intimacy vs. isolation	Love	Establish intimacy and relationships with others
Middle age 30–64 years	Generativity vs. stagnation	Care	Contribute to society and be part of a family
Old age 65 onward	Integrity vs. despair	Wisdom	Assess and make sense of life and meaning of contributions

ADULTHOOD

The relationship of the parent and child is very profound during a child's development from 0 to 18 years. According to the Danish German-American child psychoanalyst Erik Erikson, the child development stages could be divided as follows.

Stage 1. Trust Vs. Mistrust

Trust vs. mistrust is the first stage in Erik Erikson's theory of psychosocial development. According to him, the first stage begins at birth and continues to around 18 months of age. All through this stage, the infant is indeterminate about the environment in which they live, and looks towards their chief caregiver for steadiness and reliability of care. If the caregiver is consistent and nurturing, the child will grow in the feeling of trust and believes that the world it is living is a safe and secured place and people that surrounds the child are dependable and kind.

This secured feeling of trust enables the child to be protected even when it is endangered and encompasses into their other relationships, maintaining their sense of security amidst potential intimidations. Contrariwise, if the child fails to receive the consistent, satisfactory attention and affection, the child may develop a sense of mistrust and uncertainty.

This could lead to a credence in an uneven and unpredictable world, promoting a sense of distrust, suspicion, and fretfulness. In such circumstances, the child may lack self-reliance in their ability to influence events, looking the world with trepidation.

Infant Nursing

Feeding is a serious activity during this period. It's one of the basic ways that the child learns or senses whether they can place their trust in the world around. It sets the phase for their viewpoint on the world as being a safe and trustworthy place or a place of danger and extrapolation.

When a parent steadily retorts to the child's hunger by providing nourishment delicately and unfailingly, the child learns that they are cared for very well. And this in turn retaliates in their further growth, making them as people of trust and confidence.

In contrary, if a parent shows negligent attitude towards the child when it signals hunger by way of crying or seeking attention, the child may experience discomfort, distress, and hunger. This feeling in turn lead to a sense of mistrust in later stages as it leaves an impression of anxiety and insecurity for not being cared by their parents sufficiently.

Triumph and Disappointment

Victory in this stage will lead to the virtue of hope. By evolving a sense of confidence, the child can have faith that as new catastrophes rise, there is a factual likelihood that will be a way out provided by some extended hands. Failing to acquire this virtue of hope will lead to the increase of fear, where this child carries along with it a sense of mistrust in their further relationships.

Unswerving with Erikson's opinions on the prominence of trust, study by Bowlby and Ainsworth has drawn how the quality of the primary experience of a child and parent can affect dealings with others in later life.

The early stage of Erikson's stage of development makes a clear sense, it is applied well to the couples with constant marital disagreements and dissonances. Sometimes inevitably, the infancy stage is ignored or taken it for granted.

Living in an Indian culture, an explanation of why the first born is always taken care by the girl's family gave an amusing understanding of Erickson's concept of trust Vs mistrust.

During the first child birth, the woman undergoes lot of stress, anxiety and fear. In order to make the girl feel safe and secure, the tradition of making the first born child under the care of her mother came to the practice. Adding to this, the woman might feel safe and secure and can be guided the ways of nursing the child was the reason. In given atmosphere, the mother would be able to caress the newly born child taking every minute notice of the needs.

If closely observed, most of the first born were taken care by the grandparents and were given sufficient attention leading the child to grow in lot of trust and confidence. Lately, the practice of rare existing of the joint families have lagged behind a great treasure of bringing up children in an atmosphere of trust and care.

In an informal interview conducted with a newly wedded pregnant woman, it was revealed that her anxiety and stress level before giving birth was too high and added to this, she had quite few misunderstandings existed between the couples during her pregnancy period, which had left her shattered and this issues were not resolved well and unfortunately, when she gave birth to the child, she expressed, she could not feel happy at the birth of the child, that in turn raised the level of her anxiety of how is she going to bring the child up and this has created a lot of chaos in her personal life, leading disinterest in taking care of her child in the early childhood.

Sometimes, uncertain situations of life can lead to the conditions of turmoil in later stage, affecting not only the involved persons, but those around. Hence, the disputes and disagreements of parents can easily affect the child in the early stages of their life.

Stage 2. Autonomy Vs. Shame and Doubt

Autonomy Vs Shame and doubt is marked as the second stage of Erik Erikson's stages of psychosocial development. This stage befalls between the ages of 18 months to approximately 3 years. According to Erikson, children at this stage are focused on developing a sense of individual control over physical skills and a sense of freedom.

The conflict that a child can get into in this stage is Autonomy Vs Shame/doubt

If a child is fortified and reinforced in their augmented individuality, children will become more poised and sheltered in their ability to endure. They will sense a feeling of contentment in making decisions, discover their environs more spontaneously, and have a sense of self-discipline. Achieving this autonomy profits them feel capable and proficient of leading their lives.

On the other hand, if children are excessively controlled or disparaged, they may begin to feel humiliated of their autonomy and doubt their capabilities. This can lead to a lack of self-assurance, nervousness of initiating new things, and a sense of inadequacy about their willpower competences.

During this stage the child would develop physically and become more movable, realizing that he or she has many skills and abilities, such as wearing clothes and shoes, playing with toys, making their choices of food etc. Such skills prove the child's growing sense of individuality and autonomy.

For example, during this stage, children begin to affirm their independence, by walking away from their mother, alternating their mother choices with their own by picking up toys, dress, food of their choice.

Toilette Training

This is when children start to exert their independence, taking control over their bodily functions, which can greatly influence their sense of autonomy or shame and doubt. When parents approach toilet training in a patient, supportive manner, allowing the child to learn at their own pace, the child may feel a sense of accomplishment and autonomy.

They understand they have control over their own bodies and can take responsibility for their actions. This boosts their confidence, instilling a sense of autonomy and a belief in their ability to manage personal tasks. Contrariwise, if the process is rushed, if there's too much pressure, or if parents respond with anger or disappointment, the child may feel shame and start doubting their abilities. They may feel bad about their mistakes, and this can lead to feelings of shame, self-doubt, and a lack of confidence in their autonomy.

Success and Failure

Erikson states parents must allow their children to explore the limits of their abilities within an encouraging environment that is tolerant of failure. Success in this stage will lead to the virtue of **will**. If children in this stage are encouraged and supported in their increased independence, they become more confident and secure in their own ability to survive in the world. The infant develops a sense of personal control over physical skills and a sense of independence.

Suppose children are criticized, overly controlled, or not given the opportunity to assert themselves. In that case, they begin to feel inadequate in their ability to survive, and may then become overly dependent upon others, lack self-esteem, and feel a sense of shame or doubt in their abilities.

Success primes the feelings of autonomy, and failure outcomes in shame and doubt. So, the parents need to reassure the child to become more self-regulating while at the same time defending the child so that endless failure is evaded.

For example, rather than putting on the clothes, as a supportive parent have the patience to allow the child to try until they try and succeed or ask for assistance. A subtle stability is essential from the parent. They must not attempt to do all things for the child, but see if the child fails at a particular task and without disapproving the child for failures and accidents, assist the child (particularly when toilet training).

The aim has to be "self-control without a loss of self-esteem" (Gross, 1992).

The equilibrium between autonomy and shame and doubt creates understanding to the child that while they always can't s regulate their surroundings, they can implement control over their activities and choices, thus increasing self-confidence and flexibility.

Stage 3. Initiative vs. Guilt

Initiative versus guilt is the third stage of Erik Erikson's theory of psychosocial development. During this stage, children affirm themselves more frequently through directing play and other social interface.

When parents cheer and support children to take the initiative, they can start planning activities, achieve tasks, and face challenges. The children will begin to take the initiative and assert control over their given settings. They can begin to reason for themselves, formulate plans, and execute them, which helps foster a sense of purpose. If parents discourage the attainment of autonomous actions or dismiss or disapprove their efforts, children may feel guilty about their desires and initiatives.

This could potentially lead to feelings of guilt, self-doubt, and lack of initiative. These are particularly energetic, fast-developing years in a child's life. According to Bee (1992), it is a "time of vigour of action and of behaviours that the parents may see as aggressive."

In this period, the prime character includes the child commonly interrelating with other children at school. The focus of this stage is play, as it lets children to discover their interpersonal skills through initiating activities. The child begins to assert control and power over their environment by planning activities, accomplishing tasks, and facing challenges.

Exploration

Progressing Initiative: Exploration lets children to affirm their supremacy and control over their surroundings. Through exploration, children engage with their environment, raise questions, and discover new-fangled things. This dynamic engagement allows them to take the initiative and make independent choices, contributing to their autonomy and confidence.

Growing from Mistakes: Exploration also means falling and rising, making mistakes to learn from them. These provide crucial growing opportunities. Even if a child's efforts lead to errors or faults, they learn to understand reason and result and their role in influencing consequences.

Building Self-Confidence: When parents support and boost a child's explorations and initiatives, it reinforces their self-confidence. They feel their actions are respected and noteworthy, which emboldens them to take more initiative in the future.

Alleviating Guilt: If parents reverence the child's need for exploration and do not exaggeratedly complain their mistakes, it supports to avoid the feelings of blame. Instead, the child learns it's okay to try fresh things and perfectly fine to make mistakes.

Success and Failure

Children begin to plan activities, make up games, and initiate activities with others. If given this opportunity, children develop a sense of initiative and feel secure in their ability to lead others and make decisions. Success at this stage leads to the virtue of purpose.

Conversely, if this tendency is squelched, either through criticism or control, children develop a sense of guilt. The child will often overstep the mark in his forcefulness, and the danger is that the parents will tend to punish the child and restrict his initiative too much.

It is at this stage that the child will begin to ask many questions as his thirst for knowledge grows. If the parents treat the child's questions as trivial, a nuisance, or embarrassing or other aspects of their behaviour as threatening, the child may feel guilty for "being a nuisance".

Too much guilt can slow the child's interaction with others and may inhibit their creativity. Some guilt is, of course, necessary; otherwise the child would not know how to exercise self-control or have a conscience.

A healthy balance between initiative and guilt is important.

The balance between initiative and guilt during this stage can help children understand that it's acceptable to take charge and make their own decisions, but there will also be times when they must follow the rules or guidelines set by others. Successfully navigating this stage develops the virtue of purpose.

How Can Parents Encourage a Sense of Exploration?

In this stage, caregivers must provide a safe and supportive environment that allows children to explore freely. This nurtures their initiative, helps them develop problem-solving skills, and builds confidence and resilience. By understanding the importance of exploration and providing the right support, caregivers can help children navigate this stage successfully and minimize feelings of guilt.

Stage 4. Industry vs. Inferiority

Erikson's fourth psychosocial crisis involves industry (competence) vs. Inferiority which occurs during childhood between the ages of five and twelve. In this stage, children start to compare themselves with their peers to device their abilities and worth.

The Conflicts during this stage:

- **Industry**: If children are encouraged by parents and teachers to develop skills, they gain a sense of industry—a feeling of competence and belief in their skills.

  They start learning to work and cooperate with others and begin to understand that they can use their skills to complete tasks. This leads to a sense of self-confidence in their ability to achieve goals.

- **Inferiority**: On the other hand, if children receive negative feedback or are not allowed to validate their skills, they may progress a sense of inferiority.

  They may start to feel that they aren't as good as their peers or that their efforts aren't valued, leading to a lack of self-confidence and a feeling of inadequacy.

The activities during this stage:

The child begins to cope with new tasks of learning and social demands. Children at this stage start learning to read and write, to do calculations, and to do things on their own. Teachers take an important role in the child's life as they teach specific skills during this stage.

In this duration, the child's peer group will gain grander significance and become a foremost source of the child's self-esteem. The child now feels the pressure to win approval by proving specific abilities valued by society and develop a sense of satisfaction in their accomplishments.

School

This phase naturally occurs during the elementary school years, from roughly ages 6 to 11, and the experiences children have in school can significantly influence their development.

- **Development of Industry**: At school, children are provided plentiful opportunities to demonstrate their competencies, to learn and to achieve. They work on various assignments, projects, join in different activities, and collaborate with their peers, and prove their competencies.

  These experiences allow children to develop a sense of industry, strengthening their sureness in their capabilities to accomplish tasks and contribute meritoriously.

- **Social Appraisal**: The activities in the school provide a context where children can compare themselves to their peers. They gauge their abilities and achievements against those of their classmates, which can either help build their sense of industry or lead to feelings of inferiority, depending on their experiences and perceptions.

- **Feedback and Reinforcement**: Teachers play a vital role during this stage. Their feedback can either support the child's sense of industry or trigger feelings of inferiority. Reassuring feedback boosts the child's credence in their skills, while persistent negative feedback can lead to a sense of inferiority.

- **Building Life Skills**: School also provides openings for children to develop essential life skills, like problem-solving, time management, and teamwork. Successfully attaining and employing these skills promotes a sense of industry.

- **Dealing with Failure**: School is where children may encounter academic difficulties or fail for the first time, hence it becomes important that the child grows to accept failures and become emotionally stable and prepare oneself to compete.

How they learn to cope with these situations and how teachers and parents guide them through these challenges can influence whether they develop a sense of industry or inferiority.

Success and Failure in Stage Four

Success leads to the virtue of **competence**, while failure results in feelings of **inferiority**.

- If children are fortified and strengthened for their resourcefulness, they begin to feel industrious (competence) and confident in their ability to achieve goals.
- If this initiative is not appreciated and ignored, if parents or teacher limits it, then the child begins to feel deficient, doubting his/her own abilities, and therefore may not reach his or her potential.
- If the child cannot develop the specific skill they feel society demands (e.g., being athletic), they may develop a sense of Inferiority.
- Some failure may be necessary so that the child can develop some modesty. Again, a balance between competence and modesty is necessary.
- The balance between industry and inferiority allows children to recognize their skills and understand that they have the ability to work and achieve their goals, even if they face challenges along the way

Since this stage concentrates on the sagacity of exploration, the teachers and parents play a vital role in creating more consistent and constructive feedback not just considering the achievement but also acknowledging the efforts made by children.

This approach helps foster a sense of industry, competence, and confidence in children, reducing feelings of inferiority.

Stage 5. Identity vs. Role Confusion

The fifth stage of Erik Erikson's theory of psychosocial development is identity vs. role confusion. It befalls in the course of adolescence, from about 12-18 years. During this stage, adolescents search for a sense of self and personal identity, through an intense exploration of personal values, beliefs, and goals.

The conflict:

- **Identity**: If adolescents are supported in their search to find something new and given the freedom to discover different roles, they are likely to develop from this period with a strong sense of self and a feeling of independence and control.

  This process involves exploring their interests, values, and goals, which help them form their own unique identity.

- **Role Confusion**: If adolescents are restricted and not given the space to explore or find the process too overwhelming or distressing, they may experience role confusion.

  This could mean being unsure about one's place in the world, values, and future direction. They may struggle to identify their purpose or path, leading to confusion about their personal identity.

During adolescence, the transition from childhood to adulthood is most important. Children become more independent and look at the future regarding their careers, relationships, families, housing, etc. The individual wants to belong to a society and fit in.

Teenagers explore who they are as individuals, seek to establish a sense of self, and may experiment with different roles, activities, and behaviors.

According to Erikson, this is important to forming a strong identity and developing a sense of direction in life. The adolescent mind is essentially a mind or moratorium, a psychosocial stage between childhood and adulthood, between the morality learned by the child and the ethics to be developed by the adult (Erikson, 1963, p. 245).

This is a major stage of development where the child has to learn the roles he/she will occupy as an adult. During this stage, the adolescent will re-examine his identity and try to find out exactly who he or she is.

Erikson suggests that two identities are involved: the sexual and the occupational.

Social Relationships

Given the importance of social relationships during this stage, it's crucial for adolescents to have supportive social networks that encourage healthy exploration of identity.

It's also important for parents, teachers, and mentors to provide guidance as adolescents' pilot their social relationships and roles.

- **Formation of Identity**: Social relationships provide a context within which adolescents explore different aspects of their identity.

  They try on different roles within their peer groups, allowing them to discover their interests, beliefs, values, and goals. This exploration is key to forming their own unique identity.

- **Peer Influence**: Peer groups often become a significant influence during this stage. Adolescents often start to place more value on the opinions of their friends than their parents.

  How an adolescent's peer group perceives them can impact their sense of self and identity formation.

- **Social Acceptance and Belonging**: Feeling accepted and fitting in with peers can significantly affect an adolescent's self-esteem and sense of identity.

  They are more likely to develop a strong, positive identity if they feel accepted and valued. Feeling excluded or marginalized may lead to role confusion and a struggle with identity formation.

- **Experiencing Variety**: Interacting with a diverse range of people allows adolescents to broaden their perspectives, challenge their beliefs, and shape their values.

  This diversity of experiences can also influence the formation of their identity.

- **Conflict and Resolution**: Social relationships often involve conflict and the need for resolution, providing adolescents with opportunities to explore different roles and behaviors.

  Learning to navigate these conflicts aids in the development of their identity and the social skills needed in adulthood.

Success and Failure in Stage Five

According to Bee (1992), what should happen at the end of this stage is "a reintegrated sense of self, of what one wants to do or be, and of one's appropriate sex role". During this stage, the body image of the adolescent changes.

Erikson claims adolescents may feel uncomfortable about their bodies until they can adapt and "grow into" the changes. Success in this stage will lead to the virtue of fidelity.

Loyalty involves being able to commit one's self to others on the basis of accepting others, even when there may be ideological differences.

During this period, they explore possibilities and begin to form their own identity based on the outcome of their explorations.

Adolescents who establish a strong sense of identity can maintain consistent loyalties and values, even amidst societal shifts and changes.

Erikson described 3 forms of identity crisis:

1. severe (identity confusion overwhelms personal identity)
2. prolonged (realignment of childhood identifications over an extended time)
3. aggravated (repeated unsuccessful attempts at resolution)

Failure to establish a sense of identity within society ("I don't know what I want to be when I grow up") can lead to role confusion.

However, if adolescents don't have the support, time, or emotional capacity to explore their identity, they may be left with unresolved identity issues, feeling unsure about their roles and uncertain about their future.

This could potentially lead to a weak sense of self, role confusion, and lack of direction in adulthood.

Role confusion involves the individual not being sure about themselves or their place in society.

In response to role confusion or identity crisis, an adolescent may begin to experiment with different lifestyles (e.g., work, education, or political activities).

Also, pressuring someone into an identity can result in rebellion in the form of establishing a negative identity, and in addition to this feeling of unhappiness.

Stage 6. Intimacy vs. Isolation

Intimacy versus isolation is the sixth stage of Erik Erikson's theory of psychosocial development. This stage takes place during young adulthood between the ages of approximately 18 to 40 yrs. During this stage, the major conflict centres' on forming intimate, loving relationships with other people

The conflict:

- **Intimacy**: Individuals who successfully navigate this stage are able to form intimate, reciprocal relationships with others.

  They can form close bonds and are comfortable with mutual dependency. Intimacy involves the ability to be open and share oneself with others, as well as the willingness to commit to relationships and make personal sacrifices for the sake of these relationships.

- **Isolation**: If individuals struggle to form these close relationships, perhaps due to earlier unresolved identity crises or fear of rejection, they may experience isolation.

  Isolation refers to the inability to form meaningful, intimate relationships with others. This could lead to feelings of loneliness, alienation, and exclusion.

Success and Failure in Stage Six

Success leads to strong relationships, while failure results in loneliness and isolation.

Successfully navigating this stage develops the virtue of love. Individuals who develop this virtue have the ability to form deep and committed relationships based on mutual trust and respect.

During this stage, we begin to share ourselves more intimately with others. We explore relationships leading toward longer-term commitments with someone other than a family member.

Successful completion of this stage can result in happy relationships and a sense of commitment, safety, and care within a relationship.

However, if individuals struggle during this stage and are unable to form close relationships, they may feel isolated and alone. This could potentially lead to a sense of disconnection and estrangement in adulthood.

Avoiding intimacy and fearing commitment and relationships can lead to isolation, loneliness, and sometimes depression.

Stage 7. Generativity vs. Stagnation

Generativity versus stagnation is the seventh of eight stages of Erik Erikson's theory of psychosocial development. This stage takes place during middle adulthood (ages 40 to 65 yrs). During this stage, individuals focus more on building our lives, primarily through our careers, families, and contributions to society.

Here's the conflict:

- **Generativity**: If individuals feel they are making valuable contributions to the world, for instance, through raising children or contributing to positive changes in society, they will feel a sense of generativity.

  Generativity involves concern for others and the desire to contribute to future generations, often through parenting, mentoring, leadership roles, or creative output that adds value to society.

- **Stagnation**: If individuals feel they are not making a positive impact or are not involved in productive or creative tasks, they may experience stagnation.

  Stagnation involves feeling unproductive and uninvolved, leading to self-absorption, lack of growth, and feelings of emptiness.

What Happens During This Stage?

Psychologically, generativity refers to "making your mark" on the world through creating or nurturing things that will outlast an individual.

During middle age, individuals experience a need to create or nurture things that will outlast them, often having mentees or creating positive changes that will benefit other people.

We give back to society by raising our children, being productive at work, and participating in community activities and organizations. We develop a sense of being a part of the bigger picture through generativity.

Work & Parenthood

Both work and parenthood are important in this stage as they provide opportunities for adults to extend their personal and societal influence.

- **Work**: In this stage, individuals often focus heavily on their careers. Meaningful work is a way that adults can feel productive and gain a sense of contributing to the world.

  It allows them to feel that they are part of a larger community and that their efforts can benefit future generations. If they feel accomplished and valued in their work, they experience a sense of generativity.

  However, if they're unsatisfied with their career or feel unproductive, they may face feelings of stagnation.

- **Parenthood**: Raising children is another significant aspect of this stage. Adults can derive a sense of generativity from nurturing the next generation, guiding their development, and imparting their values.

  Through parenthood, adults can feel they're making a meaningful contribution to the future.

  On the other hand, individuals who choose not to have children or those who cannot have children can also achieve generativity through other nurturing behaviors, such as mentoring or engaging in activities that positively impact the younger generation.

Success and Failure in Stage Seven

If adults can find satisfaction and a sense of contribution through these roles, they are more likely to develop a sense of generativity, leading to feelings of productivity and fulfilment.

Successfully navigating this stage develops the virtue of care. Individuals who develop this virtue feel a sense of contribution to the world, typically through family and work, and feel satisfied that they are making a difference.

Success leads to feelings of usefulness and accomplishment, while failure results in shallow involvement in the world.

We become stagnant and feel unproductive by failing to find a way to contribute. These individuals may feel disconnected or uninvolved with their community and with society as a whole.

This could potentially lead to feelings of restlessness and unproductiveness in later life.

Stage 8. Ego Integrity Vs. Despair

Ego integrity versus despair is the eighth and final stage of Erik Erikson's stage theory of psychosocial development. This stage begins at approximately age 65 and ends at death. It is during this time that we contemplate our accomplishments and can develop integrity if we see ourselves as leading a successful life.

Here's the conflict:

- **Ego Integrity**: If individuals feel they have lived a fulfilling and meaningful life, they will experience ego integrity.

  This is characterized by a sense of acceptance of their life as it was, the ability to find coherence and purpose in their experiences, and a sense of wisdom and fulfilment.

- **Despair**: On the other hand, if individuals feel regretful about their past, feel they have made poor decisions, or believe they've failed to achieve their life goals, they may experience despair.

  Despair involves feelings of regret, bitterness, and disappointment with one's life, and a fear of impending death.

What Happens During This Stage?

This stage takes place after age 65 and involves reflecting on one's life and either moving into feeling satisfied and happy with one's life or feeling a deep sense of regret.

Erikson described ego integrity as "the acceptance of one's one and only life cycle as something that had to be" (1950, p. 268) and later as "a sense of coherence and wholeness" (1982, p. 65).

As we grow older (65+ yrs) and become senior citizens, we tend to slow down our productivity and explore life as retired people.

Success and Failure In Stage Eight

Success in this stage will lead to the virtue of **wisdom**. Wisdom enables a person to look back on their life with a sense of closure and completeness, and also accept death without fear.

Individuals who reflect on their lives and regret not achieving their goals will experience bitterness and despair.

Erik Erikson believed if we see our lives as unproductive, feel guilt about our past, or feel that we did not accomplish our life goals, we become dissatisfied with life and develop despair, often leading to depression and hopelessness.

This could potentially lead to feelings of fear and dread about their mortality.

A continuous state of ego integrity does not characterize wise people, but they experience both ego integrity and despair. Thus, late life is characterized by integrity and despair as alternating states that must be balanced.

Strengths And Weaknesses of Erikson's Theory

Support

1. One of the strengths of Erikson's theory is its ability to tie together important psychosocial development across the entire lifespan.

By extending the notion of personality development across the lifespan, Erikson outlines a more realistic perspective of personality development, filling a major gap in Freud's emphasis on childhood. (McAdams, 2001).

2. Based on Erikson's ideas, psychology has reconceptualised how the later periods of life are viewed. Middle and late adulthood are no longer viewed as irrelevant, because of Erikson, they are now considered active and significant times of personal growth.

3. Erikson's theory has good face validity. Many people find they can relate to his theories about various life cycle stages through their own experiences.

Criticism

Erikson is rather vague about the causes of development. What kinds of experiences must people have to successfully resolve various psychosocial conflicts and move from one stage to another? The theory does not have a universal mechanism for crisis resolution.

Indeed, Erikson (1964) acknowledges his theory is more a descriptive overview of human social and emotional development that does not adequately explain how or why this development occurs.

For example, Erikson does not explicitly explain how the outcome of one psychosocial stage influences personality at a later stage.

Erikson also does not explain what propels the individual forward into the next stage once a crisis is resolved. His stage model implies strict sequential progression tied to age, but does not address variations in timing or the complexity of human development.

However, Erikson stressed his work was a 'tool to think with rather than a factual analysis.' Its purpose then is to provide a framework within which development can be considered rather than testable theory.

Psychological Development of a child in the family

The psychological development of the child in a family, depends on factors in which the person is conditioned to live and learn. The child begins life as though it was of the mother's body. And this is seen in the child's helplessness and dependency. In the development of the child's view later, its capacities are mobilized, its ability to imagine, embroider the happenings of life, its capacity for joy, fear and freedom; its capacity for loving and need for affection, its ability to choose and being free to make choices at first seems to be freely expressed and then driven underground. (Arthur T. Jersild, Child Psychology, 1960) The child as grows in later stages if developed a healthy personality acquires realistic attitudes of self - acceptance. "She/he learns to live fairly comfortable with one's own emotions. Such persons later show the ability to assume responsibilities for their own selves. They regard themselves as someone worthy even though they are not completely perfect. They express a healthy regard for their own rights and stand up for them."

As they move towards their adulthood, they accept the limitations of their nature without feeling abused from using such resources as they are. They exhibit the capacities for right thinking, feeling and entering into friendly relationships with others. "The self- accepting person uses one's abilities, without having a compulsion to underrate them or to reach for the impossible." They learn to live as it is and don't feel the need to put on mask.

The ability to become aware of one-self is also influenced by the way one feel about oneself, the way others feel about the person and the way others express it in their actions. "To develop such an attitude, it is necessary for one to be with people, at home, or at school, or somewhere, who can help one to become aware of one's own strengths, faults, limitations without rejecting them." The family becomes an important aid for the person to develop a healthy psychology. "A self- accepting person has freedom to cultivate one's own interests without being a slave to every fad or expectation that confronts."

Sometimes families focus on physical, social or intellectual growth of the child and forget to assist them in their psychological development. It is not only necessary to provide physical and intellectual development but also to foster the emotional development. "If children are to acquire emotional maturity it is necessary for parents and teachers to allow children to show and examine their emotions." Children at their early stage learn to handle their emotions well prove to be psychologically sound. "It is essential, of course, both at home and at school to set limits beyond which a child must not go in expressing one's emotions, especially anger in an unhealthy manner."

To grow in understanding of what is important in life, a child must be encouraged to make the most important discovery of him/her. An adult having an awareness of self and have grown in a psychologically accepted conditions will express her/his willingness to receive an integrated formation. Hence, the atmosphere of family shows the great impact on the candidates' acceptance and openness to growth.

Effects of Family Economical Status

The concrete aspects of family life are closely connected with economic matters. Many point out that, to this day, the family can easily suffer from a variety of things which make it vulnerable. Among which outstanding are, low wages, unemployment, economic security, lack of decent work and a secure position at work and slavery. The above listed can have a great impact on families. Many practical aspects of a child's upbringing are influenced by one's family's socio- economic status. Sooner or later, also, a child's conception of his role in society will be influenced by the family's social, educational and economic background. "Children of low socio-economic status who live in crowded quarters in a poor neighbourhood feel the pinch in many ways. In one study parents in poor economic circumstances, in describing their relationship with their children, gave more emphasis to the physical aspects of the child care." Such children face deprivation of psychological needs to a great extent. The attention for education and other growth lacks in the low socio-economic families. This in turn affects their growth in the adulthood.

"It has been found that those of lower economic status are, on the average, more openly aggressive and more punitive in their moral attitudes, more likely to become delinquent, to have fears of a superstitious nature and also prone to many kinds of fears." Such children while growing with the same age group develop low self-esteem as they feel they are not accepted by the society because they are not able to meet the socio-economic status of the other friends. The families which do not fulfil the needs of socio-economic status of children if not given right motivation about the condition will end up in misunderstanding the capacity of parents. This may grow in them strongly as they grow in their age.

"In weighing the meaning of conduct in relation to socioeconomic status it is necessary to consider both the overt behaviour and the emotional undertones. The differences between people in the lower and middle social ranks may be more a difference in mode of expression than in intensity of feeling. Many children become more distinctly aware of status differences during the adolescence and begin to think about their vocational future.

The poor economic condition of family not only affects the comfort upbringing of the child, if later such adult joins the religious life, it may affect her/his way of thinking and acting towards poor and her own-self. The candidates of very weak and poor economic conditions without proper motivation and sound spirituality may become obstacle for the growth of others.

The unhealthy family atmosphere instils in the children a false belief system- the experiences like one is flawed and defective as a human being results in developing a false self- image. In late adolescence and early youth, with the process of discovering one's own identity, the identification with the parents' ceases for most of the adults. The learnt values from the parents become a great challenge to practice and end up in emotional disintegration.

The real struggle of youth is to grow properly. There are so many demand on them, usually imposed from parents, society, religion and the significant others in their life. All of them may mean the best for young people but the young people feel pressurised often due to the high idealism of the grownups. They feel threatened by these demands from outside. They experience a real shift in attachments and social relationships. (Shaji George and Kochuthara Viju, 2017) If a person does not understand the purpose of one's own life, one can become a threat to the society in the later years. The symptoms of an unhealthy adult who does not allow one to grow and rectify the wounds of the past in one's own life may end up in the following way of life which causes disturbance to the whole community of people around them.

- ❖ **Slipshod Mentality**: The adult takes everything as easy going task; slowly the nature of carelessness creeps within and in turn affects the growth and success rate of the person in the future.
- ❖ **Academic Excellence**: The insufficient maturity leads to less academic excellence and reverses the quality of reasoning, acting and living.
- ❖ **Restlessness:** Such a person may grow restlessness and be ruled by anxiety more than peace of mind and this may disturb the peace of the community as well.

- ❖ **Motivation:** All success and achievement may take the turn of false motivation or less motivation towards living an authentic religious life.

- ❖ **Cultural Wounds**: The respect for other's culture and richness may disappear. And such person can become the cause of division in the community.

- ❖ **Defective Habits**: unnecessary desire and irresponsible way of living may lead to defective habits like falling away from the vows.

- ❖ **Inadequate Health**-Food Habits: The demands regarding food and luxury may rise as needs above following the simple and healthy food habits.

- ❖ **No Responsible Use of Freedom**: the desire to become what one wants and impulsive behaviour may stop one to use their freedom in an irresponsible way.

- ❖ **Matters of Affectivity and Sexuality with much Cultural Sensitivity**: the problem in leading a chaste life may arise, if one is not caring and becoming a common and matured person.

- ❖ **No Understanding and Matured Growth in Psycho-Sexual Integration**: the persons with low integration often fall in the disintegrated matters on psycho-sexual problems. The main reason for this may be their earlier negligence in accepting and rectifying the unresolved childhood issues.

- ❖ **Lack of Interest in Menial and Physical Work**: The religious who fail to be formed as a healthy person treats menial and physical work as a burden. This problem is seen in a clear way in recent past among religious very much.

- ❖ **Peer Group Identification**: The dissatisfaction and the non-acceptance of oneself may lead the religious to false self -identification. This in turn may lead one to be away from the religious commitment.

Apart from the above challenges the children also may face difficulties regarding discipline, spirit of sacrifice, capacity to endure and persevere during trials and hardships.

CHAPTER VI

FAMILY THERAPY AND ADDICTION

Alcohol use is widespread, and it accounts for 3.3% of global deaths. In India, one-third of the male population consumes alcohol, and the prevalence among women is also increasing. Alcohol use disorder is characterized by persistent alcohol consumption despite experiencing harm and making multiple attempts to reduce or quit. Users often develop a tolerance, requiring progressively higher amounts for the same effect, leading to psychological and behavioral issues. Alcohol use disorder has a direct impact on mental and physical health, causing harm.

Alcohol use is common in India, with various studies indicating a prevalence of 24% to 73% among males and 24% to 45% among females in certain segments of society. In 2015, 62.5 million people in India used alcohol, with 18% of them suffering from alcohol use disorder. Alcohol-related illnesses accounted for 20-20% of hospital admissions, and this number is steadily rising due to increased alcohol consumption in India. Alcohol has resulted in numerous incurable social, physical, and psychological issues, contributing to accidents, crime, and suicide. Coping with these problems creates a nightmare for families and spouses.

In Indian villages, the impact of alcohol abuse is devastating for families. Intoxicated parents returning home often bring verbal and physical abuse, leading to repeated domestic violence. Spouses and children bear witness to this misery inflicted by their own protectors. Abuse becomes a grim part of their family life, and children learn to accept this unfortunate reality. Financial problems are another significant concern, as increased debt, mortgages, and rising loan interest rates exacerbate the misery experienced by these families.

Importance of Family therapy for Addiction

Family therapy can be instrumental in helping everyone affected by addiction understand each other, address their feelings of hurt, and navigate the complexities of maintaining a cohesive family unit. After the individual with addiction has undergone initial treatment, the family is encouraged to learn about the disease and the challenges faced by their loved one. This knowledge helps the family gain a clear understanding of appropriate and inappropriate responses to the issues related to addiction.

Once the individual has completed their in-house addiction treatment, the family can come together in a therapeutic setting to collaborate, provide motivation, and offer support, ultimately strengthening the family unit. The therapy sessions follow a semi-structured approach, covering topics such as the root causes of addiction, family dynamics, both positive and negative family responses, psychoeducation, and culminating in the development of short-term and long-term goals aimed at sobriety for the client and creating a more positive and supportive environment.

Therapists view the client as a part of a family system. In this context, when an individual is affected, the entire family is affected. Therefore, therapists work with the family to enhance relationships and address both open and hidden conflicts experienced within the family. Different schools of family therapy employ various approaches when addressing addiction within a family context. This chapter's objective is to offer a fundamental understanding of these approaches and the therapist's role in empowering families dealing with addiction.

Family system on addiction

Family systems theorists emphasize two crucial concepts: "family homeostasis" and "context." Family homeostasis refers to a situation in which the family either ignores the addictive behavior of an individual or accommodates it in order to maintain the stability of the family unit. Conversely, family dynamics can also perpetuate the addictive behaviors of the individual.

The other important concept is "context." Theorists assert that understanding an individual's behavior and addiction issues requires considering the broader family system, including the roles of the father, mother, and the system itself. Context plays a pivotal role in comprehending addictive behaviors.

When a person with addiction claims that their alcohol intake is a direct result of their spouse's actions, it is not a matter of blaming the spouse for making them an alcoholic. Rather, it highlights the interconnected nature of the family system. Addiction often arises as a consequence of the family's dynamics, not the actions of a single individual.

An integrative approach is essential for understanding the individual with addiction and all family members involved. The therapist faces the challenge of navigating a complex maze to piece together the puzzle and identify the underlying causes and the treatment process within the intricate reality of the family system, which is influenced by cultural, emotional, and psychological factors.

In family therapy, therapists aim to understand how addiction develops within the family system, its impact on the family, and the reciprocal relationship between addiction and family dynamics. This therapeutic approach involves engaging the immediate family members and focuses on altering the family dynamics that have contributed to the individual's behavioral patterns. The ultimate goal is to collaborate with the family to effect positive changes in those dynamics and interactions, with the intention of enhancing family cohesion and restoring homeostasis.

Core principles in addiction related therapy by Corless, Mirza & Steinglass (2009)

1. **Recognizing the Therapeutic Value of Working with Family Members:** Understanding that addiction often affects not only the individual but the entire family system. Involving and supporting family members in the therapeutic process can lead to better outcomes and address underlying family dynamics contributing to addiction.

2. **Incorporating a Collaborative and Non-Blaming Environment:** Fostering a safe and supportive atmosphere where individuals with addiction, their families, and therapists work together as a team. Avoiding blame and judgment helps build trust and openness in the therapeutic relationship.

3. **Applying Evidence-Based Approaches:** Utilizing evidence-based treatment methods and interventions that have proven effectiveness in addressing addiction. These approaches may include cognitive-behavioral therapy, motivational interviewing, and medication-assisted treatment, among others.

4. **Acknowledging the Importance of Relationships Within the Family and Social Networks:** Recognizing that individuals with addiction are deeply influenced by their relationships, not only within their immediate family but also within their social networks. These relationships can play a significant role in both the development and recovery from addiction. Incorporating these connections into the therapeutic process can provide valuable support and resources for the individual's recovery journey.

This principle underscores the significance of the social context and networks that individuals are part of, as they can either hinder or facilitate the recovery process. Addressing these relationships can contribute to a more comprehensive and effective approach to addiction treatment and support.

5. **Adapting the Importance of Family Counselling Methods:** Recognizing that family counselling methods are invaluable in addressing addiction issues. Incorporating family counselling into the treatment plan is essential for understanding family dynamics, improving communication, and resolving conflicts that may contribute to or result from addiction. By adapting family counselling methods, therapists can help individuals and their families work together to foster healing and recovery in a supportive and structured environment.

This principle underscores the value of specific therapeutic techniques and strategies geared towards addressing family dynamics and relationships within the context of addiction treatment. Family counselling can be a critical component of a comprehensive approach to addiction recovery.

Motivational Interviewing (MI)

MI is a client-centered, collaborative form of counselling that focuses on enhancing an individual's motivation to change. While not specifically a family therapy method, it can be adapted for use within family systems to address issues such as addiction.

In a family context, MI might involve helping family members understand their motivations for change, identify their goals, and work together to support one another in achieving those goals. It can be particularly useful when dealing with addiction issues within a family, as it helps individuals and family members explore their readiness to change and work toward recovery.

Multidimensional family therapy (MDFT)

Multidimensional Family Therapy (MDFT) is an evidence-based therapeutic approach primarily used for adolescents grappling with substance abuse and related behavioral issues. MDFT offers a comprehensive and integrative model that takes into account multiple aspects of the individual's life and relationships. Here are the general steps involved in MDFT:

1. **Assessment:** The initial step involves conducting a comprehensive assessment of the adolescent and their family. This includes gathering information about the adolescent's substance use, emotional and behavioral challenges, family dynamics, peer relationships, and any other pertinent factors.
2. **Engagement:** Therapists focus on engaging both the adolescent and their family members in the therapeutic process. Building rapport and establishing a trusting relationship are essential for effective treatment.
3. **Formulation:** A multidimensional formulation is developed based on the assessment, aiding in the identification of specific issues and dynamics within the adolescent's life. This formulation serves as a guide for the treatment plan.

4. **Individual Therapy:** The adolescent participates in individual therapy sessions, collaborating with a therapist to address personal issues, including substance abuse, emotional regulation, and problem-solving skills.

5. **Family Therapy:** Family therapy sessions serve as a central component of MDFT. These sessions aim to improve family dynamics, communication, and problem-solving skills. Family involvement plays a pivotal role in facilitating positive change in the adolescent's life.

6. **Peer and Community Interventions:** Therapists may work with the adolescent to address issues related to their peer group and community, assisting them in making positive choices regarding friends and activities.

7. **Coordination with Other Systems:** MDFT often involves coordination with other systems, such as schools, legal authorities, and healthcare providers, to ensure comprehensive support for the adolescent and a well-rounded approach to their treatment.

8. **Monitoring and Feedback:** Progress is continually monitored, and feedback is provided to the adolescent and their family, enabling the tracking of treatment effectiveness and making necessary adjustments.

9. **Relapse Prevention:** Strategies for preventing relapse are developed to help the adolescent learn how to cope with high-risk situations and avoid reverting to substance abuse and negative behaviors.

10. **Transition and Aftercare:** As the adolescent progresses in treatment, there is a focus on preparing them and their family for the transition to a less intensive level of care. Aftercare planning and support are crucial for maintaining the gains made in treatment.

11. **Graduation:** When the adolescent and their family have achieved their treatment goals and are ready to continue their progress independently, the therapy is formally concluded.

MDFT is a flexible and individualized approach, and the specific steps and interventions may vary based on the unique needs and circumstances of the adolescent and their family. It aims to address the multiple dimensions of an adolescent's life to facilitate lasting change and promote a healthy, drug-free future.

PART II

RESEARCH ON THE CAUSES OF MARITAL DISCORD

RESEARCH METHODOLOGY

AIM

- To investigate the causes of marital discord and the need for counselling among married couples in Chennai, Tamil nadu.

SPECIFIC OBJECTIVES

1. To assess the socio-demographic profile of the married couples.
2. To identify the causes of marital discord.
3. To examine the effects of marital problems on couples.
4. To assess the demand and receptivity towards counselling among couples experiencing discord.

LIMITATIONS OF THE   STUDY

1. The study lacks information on the family and social-economic background of the married couples before marriage, focusing solely on their current profile in nuclear families within their present social and economic environment.
2. The research solely represents the perspectives of the couples, excluding the opinions of other family members. The extensive and diverse nature of thoughts on this subject makes it impractical to include in this study.
3. The study does not incorporate the viewpoints of divorcees, which the researcher acknowledges as a potentially significant area of exploration deserving attention in future research endeavors.

UNIVERSE

The study focuses on the causes of marital discord and counselling needs among couples in Arul Nagar, Chennai. Arul Nagar has approximately 800 families, predominantly Tamil, residing on the north side of Chennai. The population is diverse, engaging in various professions, from daily labor to government jobs and private sector employment. The research specifically targets the Tamil population in this area.

RESEARCH DESIGN

A descriptive design is employed to identify the causes of marital discord and the need for counselling. This design allows for a quantitative exploration of existing phenomena.

SAMPLING FRAME

The study involves 50 married couples in Arul Nagar, Chennai. Married couples are considered the primary source for obtaining opinions on marital discord and counselling needs.

SAMPLING TECHNIQUE

Cluster sampling technique is utilized, where the population was divided into cluster, such as streets, and the respondents were selected randomly.

TOOLS FOR DATA COLLECTION

A questionnaire serves as the primary tool for collecting data. Ensuring anonymity and providing an opportunity for open expression. The questionnaire comprises three main components: personal profiles, marital discord inquiries, and counselling requirements.

PRE-TEST

A pre-test was conducted with two couples, resulting in questionnaire modifications and helping to establish the time frame for actual data collection.

NEED AND IMPORTANCE OF THE STUDY

Conflicts and disagreements are inevitable in every close relationship, including marital relationship. While every marriage relationship is as unique as the individuals it contains, some degree of conflict is actually necessary to keep a marriage dynamic rather than static (Ashford, LeCroy, & Lortie, 2006). Perceptions of marital quality between spouses in conflict vary. Similarly, the approaches which partners take towards handling differences vary but are crucial in determining marital satisfaction. Adjustments can be challenging because it includes adapting to myths and expectations of marriage, learning how to effectively communicate with a spouse, deriving satisfaction from the relationship and learning to deal with conflict. According to Gottman (1994), what is critical in a marriage is a balance between the couple's positive and negative interactions that determines their satisfaction. Studies have shown that failure to do so can bring detrimental effects on the mental health involving both couples and their children. As such, social support measures are extremely vital in buffering the effects of marital conflict.

ANALYSIS AND INTERPRETATION

This chapter deals with the Analysis and Interpretation of the data, the researcher also gives his insight into the interpretation of the data to give additional information towards understands the data with clarity and objectivity.

Table 1: Socio-demographic details of the Respondents

	Category	Frequency	Percentage
Age	21-30	19	38
	31-40	9	18
	41-50	15	30
	50 and above	7	14
Gender	Male	25	50
	Female	25	50
Educational Qualification	Schooling	4	8
	U.G	18	36
	P.G	20	40
	Technical	6	12
	Other	2	4
Religion	Hindu	12	24
	Muslim	0	0
	Christian	36	72
	Other	2	4

Figure 1: Occupation of the Respondents

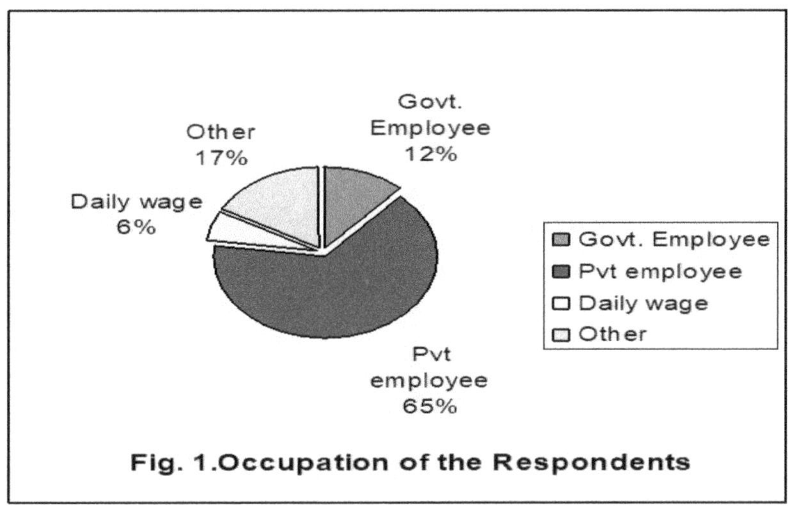

Fig. 1.Occupation of the Respondents

Table 1 the majority of respondents (65%) work in private companies. (12%) are employed in government offices or nationalized banks. (17%) are engaged in running their own small businesses, while (6%) are daily wage earners. Despite diverse occupations.

Table 2: Number of Years-Married

S. No	Years of Marriage	Frequency	Percent
1	0 -5	12	24
2	6 -10	32	64
3	11 – 15	4	8
4	20 and above	2	4
	Total	50	100

Table 2 outlines the total number of years these couples have been married. Despite facing challenges, the majority (64%) have completed five years of marriage. Additionally, 24% are in the early stages of their marriage, with only a few years or months together. A small percentage (4%) consists of couples married for over 20 years, and 8% have been married for more than a decade. The data predominantly represents the younger generation, highlighting their experiences in navigating the challenges of married life within the first few years.

Table 3: Why did you Marry?

S. No	Reason for Marriage	Frequency	Percent

1	To love & be loved	19	38
2	Security	15	30
3	Family Pressure	11	22
4	Any Other	5	10
	Total	50	100

Table 3 provides insights into the reasons behind entering into marriage. Notably, 30% of respondents married for security reasons, while a significant 22% succumbed to family or societal pressures. On a positive note, 38% sought a partner for mutual love and companionship. Additionally, 10% cited various other reasons for entering into matrimony. Understanding these motivations is crucial, as marriages founded on consent and shared affection may be more resilient than those influenced by external pressures.

Table 4: Do both the partners work?

S. No	Do Both of you work?	Frequency	Percent
1	Yes	38	76
2	No	12	24

	Total	50	100

Table 4 reveals that 76% of respondents have both partners working and sharing household responsibilities, challenging traditional breadwinner roles. In 24% of cases, one partner works while the other is a homemaker, emphasizing diverse household arrangements. The data reflects evolving societal norms regarding work and domestic roles.

Table 5: Monthly Income

S. No	Monthly Income	Frequency	Percent
1	Less than 10,000	10	20
2	10,001-20,000	32	64
3	20,001-25,000	4	8
4	25,000 and above	4	8
	Total	50	100

Table 5 reveals that the majority of respondents earn between 10,000 to 20,000 rupees per month, a common income range for individuals working in private sectors in Chennai. Notably, 20% earn below 10,000 rupees, facing the challenges associated with financial difficulties. The researcher observes that financial strain can contribute to marital discord. Additionally, 16% of respondents earn a substantial amount suitable for a middle-class family. Interestingly, even among this group, finance is a contributing factor to conflict, but more severe family issues also play a significant role in family discord.

Table 6: Was your Marriage Arranged?

SL. No	Arranged Marriage	Frequency	Percent
1	Yes	46	92
2	No	4	8
	Total	50	100

Table 6 underscores the prevalent practice of arranged marriages in our state and country. A substantial majority, around 92% of respondents, reported that their marriages were arranged by their parents or guardians, with the consent of the couples, though decisions were often made after consulting the individuals involved. Notably, the majority did not have the option to reject the arrangement. In contrast, a minority of 8% either married with or without parental consent, highlighting the existence of alternative marriage arrangements beyond the traditional practice.

Table 7: Visit to a Counsellor

S. No	Visited a Counsellor	Frequency	Percent
1	No	38	76
2	Yes	12	24
	Total	50	100

Table 7 explains the taboo of visiting the counsellor in their area, some of the respondents who belong to the Christian religion have met their clergy men but they have not even heard about the counsellor for these problems. Many of the respondents said that nothing could be done about the problem and it was their fate and they have to suffer silently and not seek help at all from anybody. A majority of 76 percent respondents have not visited a counsellor or a helper during the time of marriage but while the 24 percent of the respondents have received some kind of help from their respective authority in order to solve their marital issues.

Causes of Marital Conflict

Table 8: Understand Each other's Feelings

S. No	Understand Each other's Feelings	Frequency	Percent
1	Never	10	20
2	Once in while	14	28
3	Sometimes	16	32
4	Frequently	8	16
5	Almost Always	2	4
	Total	50	100

Table 8 highlights a key factor in marital breakdown: a lack of understanding. Notably, 20% of respondents feel their partners never understand them. While 80% make efforts to understand each other, only 4% claim to consistently grasp their partner's feelings. The data underscores the crucial role of understanding in marital relationships.

Table 9: Get your points across without Trouble

S. No	Get your points Across	Frequency	Percent
1	Never	5	10

2	Once in while	12	24
3	Sometimes	13	26
4	Frequently	20	40
5	Almost Always	0	0
	Total	50	100

Table 9 indicates the effectiveness of communication between couples. Notably, 40% of respondents frequently share their points of view successfully, while 26% do so sometimes. However, 24% encounter difficulty, managing to communicate only occasionally. The data also reveals that 10% find it utterly impossible to share their perspectives, signaling a breakdown in communication that hinders marital growth and change.

Table 10: Do you appreciate Each other?

S. No	Do you appreciate Each other?	Frequency	Percent
1	Never	2	4
2	Once in a while	15	30
3	Sometimes	22	44
4	Frequently	10	20
5	Almost Always	1	2

	Total	50	100

Table 10 identifies a significant factor contributing to family conflict: a failure to appreciate one another. Only 44% of respondents appreciate each other sometimes, and 30% do so once in a while. Notably, 20% express appreciation only when prompted, revealing a potential source of family conflicts. A small minority (4%) never receive any appreciation, underscoring its impact on relationship building, creating a sense of distaste and a lack of togetherness in marital life.

Figure 2: Supportive of One Another's Feelings

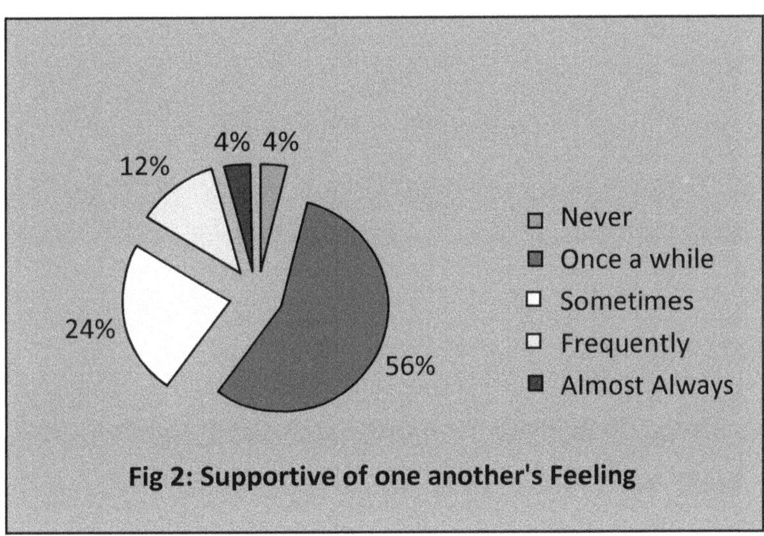

Figure 2 illustrates the support married couples provide to each other, particularly in expressing feelings, a crucial aspect of marital life. The majority (56%) feel their partners are very supportive occasionally. Additionally, 24% provide support sometimes, 12% frequently, while 4% never perceive support from their counterparts. These findings underscore the importance of emotional support in enhancing marital well-being.

Table 11: Does your husband/wife tell you not to feel that way about the issue?

S. No	Feeling about the issue	Frequency	Percent
1	Never	0	0
2	Once in while	26	52
3	Sometimes	14	28
4	Frequently	4	8
5	Almost Always	6	12
	Total	50	100

Table 11 reveals a notable gap in responding to each other's feelings on various issues among respondents. A concerning 52% provide help once in a while, posing challenges in long-term relationships. Additionally, 28% assist at times, while a positive 20% offer frequent or almost constant support. It's encouraging that none reported never helping, emphasizing the importance of addressing important issues for the growth of marital relations.

Table 12: Is your husband/wife willing to hear you?

S. No	Willing to hear	Frequency	Percent
1	Never	4	8
2	Once in while	14	28
3	Sometimes	20	40
4	Frequently	8	16
5	Almost Always	4	8
	Total	50	100

Table 12 highlights the crucial skill of listening in marital relationships. 40% of respondents sometimes listen to each other's views, fostering willingness to hear different perspectives. 28% do so occasionally, while a notable 16% frequently engage in active listening. Only 8% always listen, and another 8% never do, emphasizing the need for moderation in communication for marital harmony.

Figure 3: Does your husband / Wife contradict your ideas?

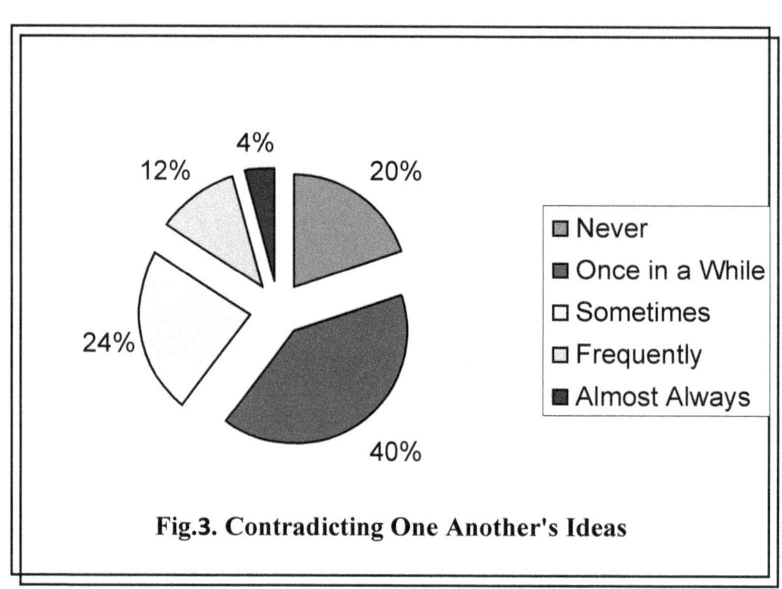

Fig.3. Contradicting One Another's Ideas

Figure 3 reveals the attitude of the married couples especially on contradicting one another's ideas before even listening to each other. Even though it shows the amount respect and love, they have for each other. If there is lack of respect for the counter part then other person's ability to propose an idea would automatically be opposed. The figure clearly throws light that 44 percent of the respondents never contradict one another's ideas before listening to each other and this seems a very good trend among the couples, but 24 percent of the Respondents do contradict one another at least sometimes, but only a very few percent of 4 percent always contradict the other's idea without even listening to one another. Contradicting one another's ideas without even listening to them can add more fuel to family problems.

Table 13: Are your Views important to your husband/wife?

S. No	Are your views important?	Frequency	Percent
1	Never	5	10
2	Once in while	12	24
3	Sometimes	26	52
4	Frequently	6	12
5	Almost Always	1	2
	Total	50	100

Table 13 shows the importance that the couples give to one another's view especially when the view is listened to and analyzed. 52 percent of the Respondents clearly state that sometimes they give importance to the counterpart, while about 24 percent of the Respondents give importance to the other's view only once in a while, and 12 percent of the Respondents frequently give importance to other's view, but only 2 percent always give importance to the other's view and 10 percent of the Respondents never give any importance what so ever to the view of the counterpart, but the sad part is that there is no frequent respect and importance given to one another, but it's always sometimes or once in a while.

Table 14: Does your husband/wife try to always justify his/her point of view?

SL. No	Attempt to justify one's view	Frequency	Percent
1	Never	10	20
2	Once in while	14	28
3	Sometimes	16	32

4	Frequently	8	16
5	Almost Always	2	4
	Total	50	100

Table 14 aims to show the attitude of the husband / wife in trying to justify always his / her point of view. The majority of the Respondents that is 32 percent sometimes try to justify their point of view, 28 percent of the Respondents justify their views with all kinds of excuses and arguments. Whereas 20 percent of the Respondents never try to justify but rather get into discussion in order help one another to reach a common ground in diverging point of views. The disturbing factor is that 16 percent of the Respondents frequently justify his / her point of view, and 4 percent always justify.

Table 15: Does your husband / wife let you to be angry without putting you down?

SL. No	Space to express your emotion	Frequency	Percent
1	Never	6	12
2	Once in while	12	24
3	Sometimes	20	40
4	Frequently	4	8
5	Almost Always	8	16

	Total	**50**	**100**

Table 15 shows the ability to express emotion in front of each other, without being humiliated or put down. It is good to express our emotions especially anger in opt way possible in the presence of the counterpart. But sometimes it could also make them vulnerable, that the other ridicules the expression as childish, or unlearned or lacks ability to guard emotions. But it's good to note that 12 percent of the Respondents never put down their counterpart for expressing their emotion. But 24 percent of the respondents provide enough space to express their emotion only once in a while and a whopping 40 percent provide enough space to express their feelings sometime and a good number of respondents that is 16 percent of the respondents almost always provide space to express their emotion and never put down their counterpart.

Table 16: Does your husband / wife blame you for everything?

SL. No	Blame For everything	Frequency	Percent
1	Never	2	4
2	Once in while	14	28
3	Sometimes	16	32
4	Frequently	2	4
5	Almost Always	16	32
	Total	**50**	**100**

Table 16 expresses the attitude of the couples to blame the counterpart for everything and anything. The 32 percent of the Respondents say that they always blame their counterpart for all their problems, and another 32 percent express that they sometimes blame the other for everything, and 28 percent blame once in a while, and just 4 percent of the Respondents never blame the counterpart for his / her problem. The researcher wants to make an important observation here, that most of the Respondents are not willing to take responsibility for their own problems and issues, and rather they have a habit of blaming the other for everything. This is very prominent among the respondents, a huge number of respondents that is about 96 percent of the Respondents some time or the other blame the counter part for everything that has happened in their life time.

Figure 4: Financial problems

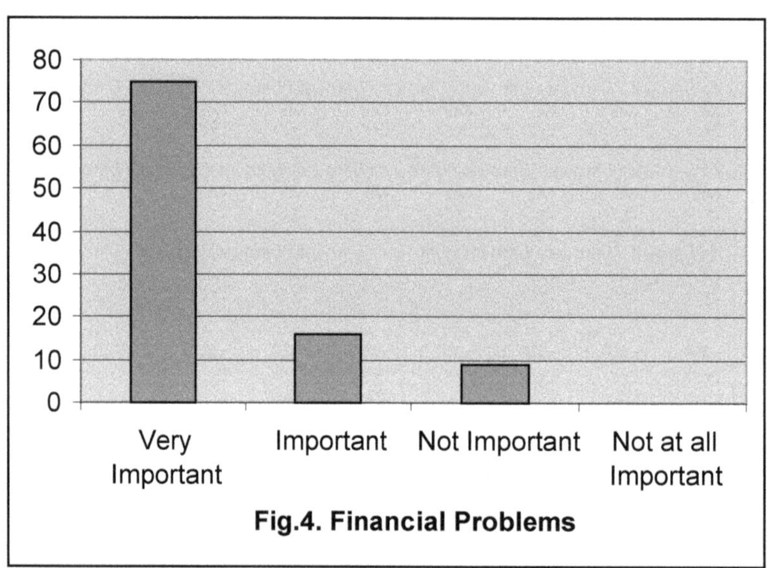

Figure 4 reveals the other causes for marital discord, the researcher has put financial problems as the first question, as it plays a vital importance in leading to marital discord in families especially in our society today. As expected by the researcher, majority of 76 percent of the Respondents say that finance is very important in avoiding marital discord in the family today and 14 percent of the Respondents reveal that financial problems its important factor that contributes to martial conflicts but its not vital important, just 8 percent of the Respondents state that financial problems are not important in marital conflicts and a meager 2 percent of the Respondents just do not care for cash in their family relations. The researcher found that most of the Respondents belong to the middle class and they value money because without a substantial amount, it is not easy to respond to the eventualities of this time.

Table 17: **Unfaithful Affair (Infidelity)**

SL. No	Infidelity	Frequency	Percent
1	Very Important	44	88
2	Important	4	8
3	Not important	2	4
4	Not at all important	0	0
	Total	**50**	**100**

Table 17 explains one of the major causes that can lead to marital discord, is the infidelity of the Husband / wife. In our society even though, extra marital affairs are a taboo, extra marital affair seems to be rampant in our society. How ever the seriousness of the mistake is not excused among the marital couples. A whopping majority of 88 percent consider infidelity as one of the major causes for marital discord and that could lead to you deeper argument and division among the couple, when the extra marital is found, there will be a crack in their relationship. Another 8 percent of the Respondents consider that it is also important for marital conflicts. But its also astonishing that in our culture, some have become so lenient that they consider it to be not important in creating marital discord.

Table 18: Suspicion & Jealousy

SL. No	Suspicion & Jealousy	Frequency	Percent
1	Very Important	36	72
2	Important	10	20
3	Not important	4	8
4	Not at all important	0	0
	Total	**50**	**100**

Table 18 draws our attention on suspicion and Jealousy between the husband and the wife. If a husband or wife is suspicious about one another then their intimacy is so disturbed that they begin to fall apart emotionally. Thus, a majority of 72 percent of the Respondents believe that suspicion could play an important role in family discord, it could lead to arguments, fights and division between the couples. And 20 percent of the Respondents also believe that suspicion and jealousy is important in creating family discord. Only a surprising 4 percent of the respondents believe it may not be important especially in emotional unity between the husbands and the wives. But the majority 92 percent believe that it could play a vital role in marital discord.

Table 19: Sexual Difficulties

L No		Frequency	Percent
1	Very Important	22	44
2	Important	16	32
3	Not important	12	24
4	Not at all important	0	0

	Total	50	100

Table 19 reveals the difficulties rising in the sexual intimacy, even though our society is shy to talk openly about the sexual difficulties and the need for sexual intimacy, the Respondents seem to have given a fair verdict especially on the aspects of sex and intimacy among the married couples. A good majority of 44 percent of the Respondents believe that sexual difficulties could play a vital role in marital discord. While 32 percent of the Respondents believe it is important and a good 22 percent believe it is not important thing and we should not consider it, as one of the major causes that creates marital discord among the married couples. Indian are slowly waking up to understanding sexuality and sexual intimacy, and they have a right to believe that sexual difficulties could also bring in marital discord.

Figure 5: Physical Abuse

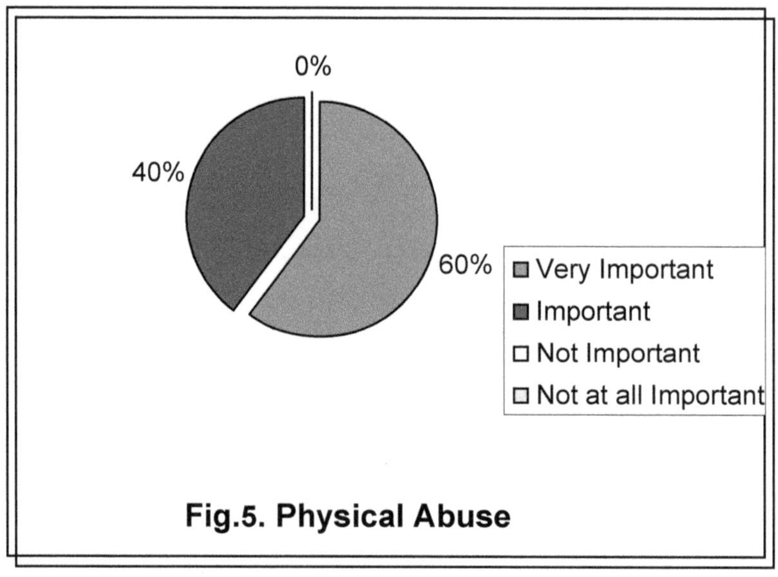

Fig.5. Physical Abuse

Figure 5 explains the physical Abuse as another major cause for marital discord; it's well known that domestic violence has shown its horror face in our cities and especially cities. The weight of the patriarchal nature of our society is a burden to our women; they are suppressed, ill-treated and un-respected. The Researcher from this questionnaire has found that domestic violence or physical abuse is not accepted at all in our modern families, working women are strong about this attitude and this is a welcome step in our country. A complete 100 percent of the respondents believe that physical abuse, as one of the major causes for marital breakdown.

Table 20: Sexual Abuse

SL. No	Infidelity	Frequency	Percent
1	Very Important	12	24
2	Important	20	40
3	Not important	12	24
4	Not at all important	6	12

	Total	50	100

Table 20 expresses that Sexual Abuse as one of the causes for marital breakdown, even though Indian men and women do not experiment with sex because they lack enough space and privacy to carry on experiments in general. But there is always a lot of news about women being treated as a sex slave within the ambit of marriage. Even though Indian women do not openly talk about such happening outside the four walls of bed room. The modern couples support sexual need as well as sexual freedom in the commitment. A majority of 40 percent of the Respondents say that it is important to marital discord, while 24 percent confirm that it is very important cause. But the is also enough number of Respondents that is 24 percent feel it is not important and should be borne silently by the victim, and surprisingly 12 percent believe it is not at all important cause for marital break down.

Table 21: Verbal Abuse

SL. No	Verbal Abuse	Frequency	Percent
1	Very Important	10	20
2	Important	18	36
3	Not important	18	36
4	Not at all important	4	8
	Total	50	100

Table 21 reveals Verbal Abuse not as another important cause of marital breakdown. In our society, there seems to be unbearable verbal abuse on the couples and especially on the weaker section of our society. Yet our society men and women especially begin adjust with such realities; It seems that there are many other important issues and this does not hold enough water. Even though 36 percent of the Respondents say that it is important cause of marital discord and another 36 percent of the Respondents believe that it is not important cause of marital breakdown, obviously it could be borne with. While 20 percent of the Respondents believe that it is very important and 8 percent of the Respondents believe it is not at all important in building marital discord.

Figure 6: Alcohol Abuse

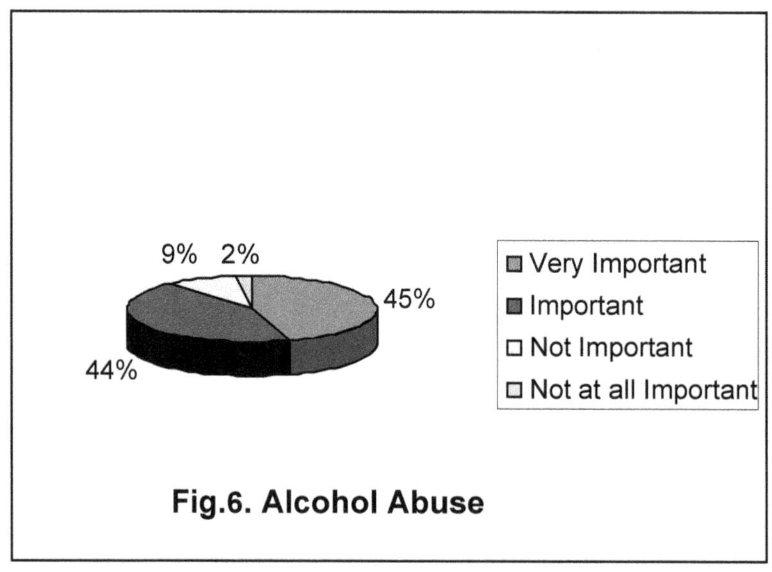

Figure.6. explains that Alcohol Abuse could be one of the major causes for marital fight and discord. There is rampant alcohol problem among men in India, the influence of alcohol leads to a variety of problems such as disinterested in family activities, children, and occupation or in

social relationship within the family circle. Alcohol Abuse has direct influence on the children and the reputation of the family among the neighbours. A great majority of 89 percent of the Respondents reveal that it plays a vital role in marital conflict and discord. When a husband/wife begins to abuse alcohol, it brings other problems such as health hazard and sexual difficulties so on and so forth. Just a meager 10 percent of the Respondents believe that it is not important and a dismissible 2 percent of the Respondents say that it is not an important cause at all for marital conflicts and problems.

Table 22: **Difference of Interest**

SL. No	Alcohol Abuse	Frequency	Percent
1	Very Important	8	16
2	Important	12	24
3	Not important	28	56
4	Not at all important	2	4
	Total	**50**	**100**

Table 22 reveals another dimension of our cultural thinking, that difference of interest has to be tolerated. There seems to be less individual interest in our society, the women carry out their house hold duties even when they are disinterested, ill or even when consider it as a burden. The men stay in their jobs irrespective of their interest for decades. The Respondents keeping that cultural anomaly in their mind said that 56 percent believe that it is not important cause for marital conflict, while 24 percent believe that it is important and just 16 percent believe that it is a very important cause for marital conflict. While 4 percent of the Respondents believe it is not at all an important cause for marital discord in our families.

Figure 7: Occupational Issues

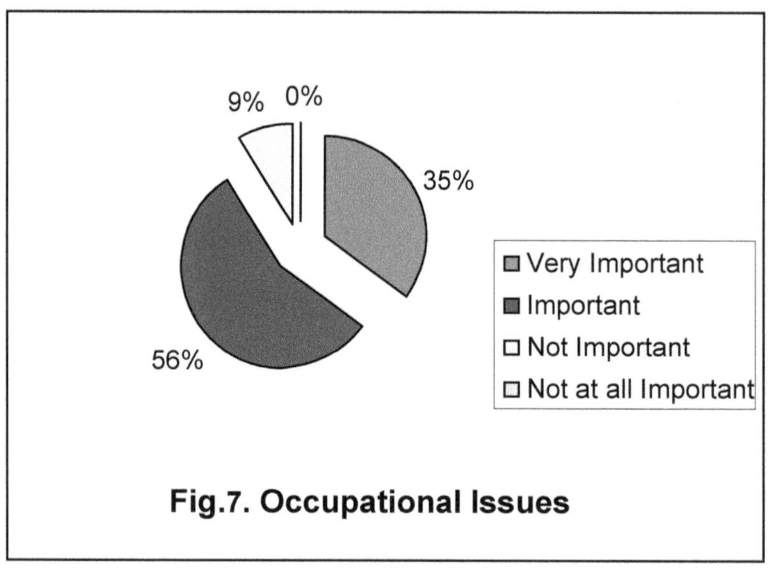

Fig.7. Occupational Issues

Figure. 7 reveals that the 56 percent of the Respondents believe that occupation is very important otherwise it could bring a big crisis in family lives and 35 percent of the Respondents give an ultimate importance to occupation, that it is very important otherwise it could be a major cause lading to marital discord. Today it's very important to be in a good business in order to support your family financially as well as to have a status in our society. It uplifts the morale of the family members as well as gives them an identity to live their lives with dignity. Therefore, a whopping majority of 91 percent of the Respondents say that occupation and occupational issues are very important causes for marital discord among the married couples.

Table 23: Too Much Interference from In-laws

SL. No	Interference from In-laws	Frequency	Percent
1	Very Important	14	28
2	Important	6	12
3	Not important	26	52

4	Not at all important	4	8
	Total	**50**	**100**

Table 23 explains that unnecessary interference from other relatives (such as in-laws) could also play a vital role in marital conflict, but since our respondents are mostly living in nuclear families, they seem to be, not having a serious problem of interference into their marital lives and dictating terms to them. It is a serious problem in villages, where the relatives live together either in a joint family or in a close circle. A majority of 52 percent of the Respondents say that it is not an important problem that causes marital conflict, whereas 28 percent believe that it is very important and 12 percent say that it is an important cause of marital discord among couples.

Table 24: Is Seeking help a taboo in our society?

SL. No	Seeking Help a Taboo?	Frequency	Percent
1	Yes	38	76
2	No	12	24
	Total	**50**	**100**

Table 24 explains an awkward reality of our society. That the married couples who are in conflict and discord refuse to seek help because seeking help especially from a professional family therapist or a relational counsellor is considered a taboo in our society. The relatives don the role of family therapist and try to help them to stay together without even solving their problems. While 24 percent of the Respondents say that it is not a taboo to seek help, when the marriage is going down the drain. The researcher found that the Respondents, even though educated, fall in line with a primitive thinking of refusing to seek help.

Figure 8: Do you Seek help?

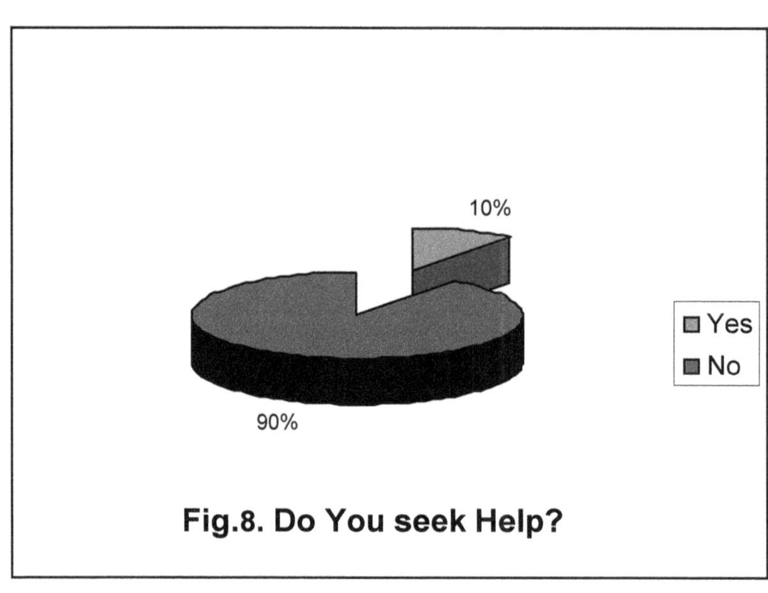

Fig.8. reveals even though 24 percent of Respondents believe that seeking help is not a taboo in our society, yet when it comes to seeking help only 10 percent of the Respondents seek help, while a disturbing percentage of 90 percent of the Respondents do not seek help from any body to solve their problems. This belief is based on the presupposition that seeking help is a taboo and hence it should not be encouraged in our marital disputes, rather the others should forcefully enter into helping them even without their consent.

Table 25: Will you accept the Role of a Counsellor?

SL. No	Accept the Role of a Counselor?	Frequency	Percent

1	Yes	35	70
2	No	15	30
	Total	**50**	**100**

Table 25 explains whether the Respondents will accept the role of a Counsellor in helping them to realize the issues and paving the way for resolution of differences among the couples. Even though there are not many who will be visiting the counsellor for the marital discord but a surprisingly 70 percent of the Respondents are ready and willing to accept the role of a counsellor in order to resolve the difference between the married couples. But the other 30 percent of the Respondents are not even willing to accept the Role of the counsellor in helping them to resolve their difference. There seems to be a vast lack of acceptance even in accepting the help provided to help themselves. This is keeping with a view that seeking help is a sign of weakness in our society.

Figure 9: Do you wish to change your Partner?

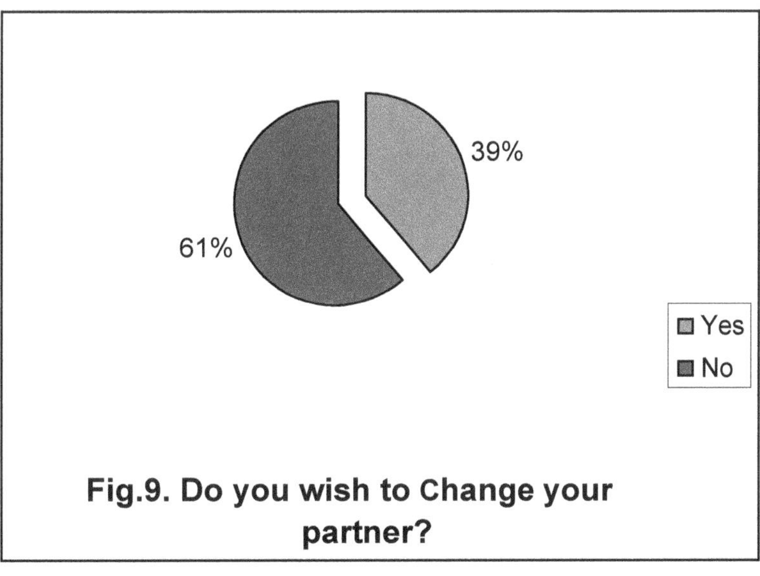

Fig.9 reveals the desire to change the partner because of the strong belief that other is the cause of the problem. But on the contrary, seeking a counselor is not to change the other but to change one self. But a majority of the Respondents that is 61 percent of them believe that they do not wish to change their partner rather aim at self-change. And the rest of the Respondents that is about 39 percent of them wish to change their partner because they wish to make their relation more meaningful and help one another to change their marital reality. The researcher has found that most people tend to believe that the other is the causes for their marital problem and not even wishing to change oneself for a better relationship.

Table 26: Will you walk out of Marriage?

SL. No	Will you walk out of Marriage?	Frequency	Percent
1	Yes	6	12
2	No	44	88
	Total	**50**	**100**

Table 26 reveals the respondents are willing to hold on to their partner even when there is discord among themselves. Even though our culture does not give an option of walking out of marriage or get a divorce like a western trend. Yet the Respondents, keeping to the tradition of Indian custom and culture have answered in a more opt manner. A vast majority of 88 percent of the Respondents have said that they will not walk out of marriage at any time. But a good 12 percent of the Respondents have said, if there are too many difficulties coming their way, they are willing to walk out of marriage.

Figure 10: can all marital problems be solved?

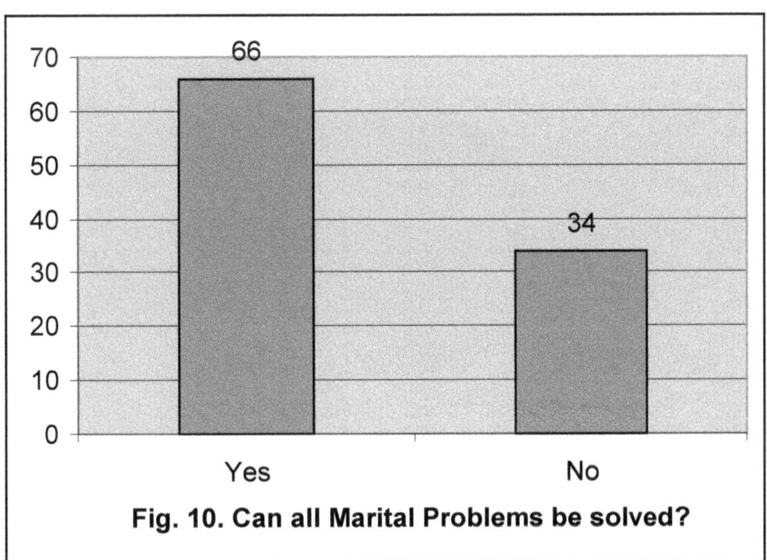

Fig. 10. Can all Marital Problems be solved?

Figure 10 explains the attitude of the Respondents towards solving their marital Problems. The question aims to discover whether all marital problems can be solved. A good majority of 66 percent have responded that they believe all marital problems could be solved by right approach and timely help. But surprisingly 34 percent of the Respondents believe that all marital problems be solved. If the Respondent believes that every problem has a solution than the Respondent begins to work at arriving at their solution with the help of competent people.

Figure 11: Is love enough for Marriage?

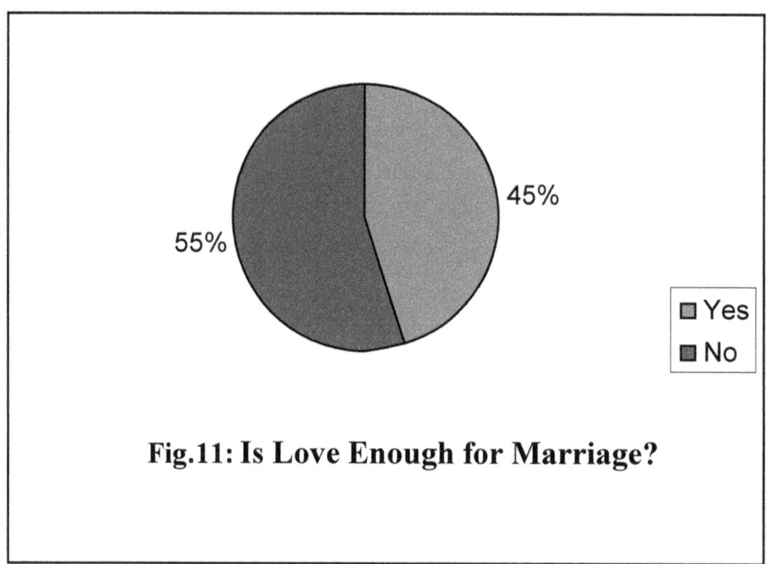

Fig.11: Is Love Enough for Marriage?

Figure11 there are so many love marriages in our society, which ends up in divorce. It clearly explains that love is not going to keep the marriage. Even though love is the basis of marriage, yet that love has to mature on so many aspects of human living. Initial bliss of love will slowly disappear paving the path towards more emotional, physical stability between each other. But the 45 percent of the respondents still believe that love is enough for marriage. But the majority of 55 percent of the Respondents have said love alone is not enough in a marital bond and there are other requirements that make a marital bond complete between the couples.

Self-Reflection Questions for Marriage Recovery

Before embarking on a marriage recovery strategy, it is crucial to ask yourself the following questions:

1. Am I ready and willing to improve the situation?
2. Do I feel deep in my heart that my marriage is worth it?
3. Am I willing to put in the effort to apply strategies to solve my marital problems?

Answering these questions positively is the first step on the road to recovery. With a commitment to improving your relationship, you can then follow specific strategies designed to resolve any marital conflicts you may face.

Restoring Love versus Resolving Conflicts

The researcher proposes a new paradigm for restoring love among couples. This method has been utilized by many relationship counsellors and family therapists. The researcher finds that focusing on restoring love, rather than merely resolving conflicts, leads to the automatic resolution of conflicts. The following methods are recommended for couples working through marital issues, based on both the researcher's findings and personal experiences with marital discord.

If you've seen a marriage counsellor and were disappointed with the results, it might be because you focused on resolving conflicts rather than restoring love. Even if you made progress in resolving conflicts, you may still have felt unhappy in your marriage. This highlights a key issue with popular approaches to marital therapy: resolving conflicts alone often fails to save marriages. When conflict resolution goals are achieved in counselling, why do couples still divorce? This suggests that there is more to a successful marriage than just resolving conflicts.

The researcher acknowledges the importance of conflict resolution in marriage and that counsellors work hard to help couples with this. However, happily married couples do more than resolve conflicts—they also preserve their feelings of love for each other. Without love, marriage feels incomplete. When couples seek counselling, they often present a list of unresolved conflicts, but their greatest despair typically stems from lost feelings of love and passion. They may believe that these feelings will never return and, without them, they no longer want to stay married. Therefore, the greatest source of hopelessness is often the loss of love, not the inability to resolve conflicts.

The researcher learned early in his career that restoring love is far more important than resolving conflicts. To be completely happy, couples must rediscover their love for each other. Dr. William Harley, a family counsellor introduced the concept of the "Love Bank" to illustrate how love is created and destroyed in relationships. Every action either deposits or withdraws love units.

Since most actions are habitual, habits play a crucial role in maintaining or eroding love. The feeling of love can last a lifetime if couples follow two simple rules: 1) avoid withdrawing love units and 2) keep depositing them. Maintaining a positive Love Bank balance above the romantic love threshold is essential.

Steps to Building Romantic Love:

1. **Commit to Building Romantic Love**: Problems are not solved by chance; they are created by chance. To keep love in your marriage, you must commit to this purpose. The "Agreement to Overcome Love Busters and Meet the Most Important Emotional Needs" form outlines the steps needed to guarantee romantic love.

2. **Identify Destructive Habits**: It's pointless to build romantic love if destructive habits persist. The "Analysis of Love Busters Questionnaire" helps identify these habits, which undermine efforts to build love.

3. **Eliminate Love Busters**: Create and execute a plan to eliminate the identified Love Busters. The workbook provides inventories, strategies, and worksheets to systematically overcome these habits. The most common Love Busters—anger, disrespect, and demands—are instinctive but destructive approaches to conflict resolution. Effective conflict resolution should consider both spouses' interests and feelings. Abandoning negative habits makes conflicts easier to resolve while maintaining love.

4. **Identify Emotional Needs**: The way to deposit the most love units is by meeting the most important emotional needs. The "Analysis of Emotional Needs Questionnaire" helps couples identify and communicate these needs.

5. **Meet Emotional Needs**: Learn to meet the identified needs. The workbook provides detailed methods for meeting the ten most common emotional needs. Forms and worksheets help plan and document progress toward meeting these needs.

Completing these five steps will help you create and implement a plan to restore love in your marriage. If you struggle to follow the program, consider seeking a therapist's guidance. Bring the workbook to your therapy sessions to ensure you stay on track.

Negotiating Conflicts with Love

Restoring and sustaining romantic love also transforms conflict resolution. You will seek solutions that deposit love units into both Love Banks simultaneously. Solutions that make one spouse happy at the other's expense (win-lose) will not build love. Instead, you will negotiate until you find mutually agreeable solutions (win-win). This approach ensures both partners deposit love units whenever a problem is solved.

Sustaining Romantic Love

Sustained romantic love is a testament to your care and protection of each other. Care means meeting each other's important emotional needs, while protection means considering each other's feelings in daily actions. Your marriage will be passionate and fulfilling if both you and your spouse commit to a plan that guarantees care and protection. The effort is well worth it.

Epilogue

"People want their relationship to work, but they don't want to work for their relationship"

The western influence in our society, the increase in earning power, lack of adjustment, enlargement of ego and individualism is playing a crucial role in family conflicts yet the Respondents strongly believe that they have to work towards making their marriages work. The majority of 88 percent of the Respondents clearly state that they will not walk out of marriage at any circumstance. It might be because of social stigma or security reasons but yet there is always a pull to live with their partners. The respondents clearly state the causes of marital conflict and the need for counselling in order to solve their marital issues.

The following major causes have been identified by the researcher for the marital conflict; they are infidelity (88%), financial problems (76%), suspicion and jealously (72%), Physical Abuse (60%), occupational issues (56%), difference in interest (56%) and interference from in-laws (52%). These causes create havoc in their family relations. The researcher found that the couples are clearly aware of the causes of marital conflict yet these seem to be the said causes, but the real difficulty begins with the failure in communication and lack of other-consciousness among the couple.

The researcher strongly believes that the study cannot reveal something extremely new, but a glance in to the lives of married couples are of utmost importance to help them to see their "human-face" the real that they are. And to seek help in time of need. The surprising find of the research is that the majority of the Respondents (76 percent) still believe that it is taboo to seek professional help in times of marital discord and another disappointing find in this research is that 90 percent of the Respondents do not seek help in troubled times of their marital lives. The researcher found the study, more appealing to the married couple yet this type of research undertaking will bring awareness to the married couples about the importance of seeking help in times of marital discord.

As we conclude "Marital Discord and Family Therapy," it is essential to reflect on the journey we have undertaken. We have explored the complexities of marital conflicts, the underlying causes, and the profound impact they have on families. Through the lens of family therapy, we have examined various strategies and interventions that can heal wounds, rebuild trust, and restore harmony within the household. The stories and case studies presented in this book highlight the resilience and strength of individuals and couples facing marital discord. They demonstrate that, despite the challenges, effective communication, empathy, and professional guidance can lead to meaningful transformation.

Family therapy is not a one-size-fits-all solution. It requires a tailored approach that considers the unique dynamics of each family. By embracing these principles, couples can navigate their conflicts with a renewed sense of understanding and commitment.

As you close this book, remember that the path to resolution and reconciliation is ongoing. Marital discord may be a part of the journey, but it does not define the destination. With dedication, patience, and the right support, families can emerge stronger and more united.

Thank you for joining us on this exploration of marital discord and family therapy. May the insights gained here inspire hope, foster growth, and encourage lasting change in your own relationships and those around you.

Acknowledgments

We extend our deepest gratitude fr. Gabriel Mathias ofm for proof reading and the support and contribution by Ms. Shilpa in editing and reviewing and also to all the therapists, researchers, and families who contributed to this work. Your experiences and expertise have enriched our understanding and provided invaluable lessons for all readers.

REFERENCES

Ables, B., & Brandsma, J. (1977). *Therapy for couples*. Jossey-Bass Publishers, San Francisco, 45-60.

Around, & S. L. Pauker. (1987). *The first year of marriage*. Warner Books, New York, 75-115.

Ashford, J., LeCroy, C. W., & Lortie, K. L. (2006). *Human behavior in the social environment: A multidimensional perspective*. Wadsworth Publishing, Belmont, 24-38.

Bowen, M. (1978). *Family therapy in clinical practice*. Jason Aronson, New York, 103-145.

Olson, D. H., & DeFrain, J. (1994). *Marriage and the family: Diversity and strengths*. Mayfield Publishing Company, London, 25-425.

Von Hildebrand, D. (1966). *Man and woman*. Franciscan Herald Press, Illinois, 75-83.

De Smedt, E. J. (1963). *Married love*. Geoffrey Chapman, London, 11-72.

Folger, J. P., & Poole, M. S. (1984). *Working through conflict*. Scott, Foresman and Co., Glenview, Illinois, 11-42.

Folkman, S., & Lazarus, R. S. (1991). *Coping and emotion*. Columbia University Press, New York, 207-227.

Piercy, F. P., & Sprenkle, D. H. (1986). *Family therapy sourcebook*. The Guilford Press, New York, 25-44.

Hornstein, G. A., & Faller, L. H. (1964). *Sex and marriage*. Popular Library Books, New York, 57-138.

Dominian, J. (1984). *Marriage, faith and love*. Fount Paperbacks, London, 107-124.

Bird, J., & Bird, L. (1983). *To live as family: An experience of love and bonding*. Image Books, New York, 31-49.

Ronch, J. L., Van Ornum, W., & Stilwell, N. C. (1994). *The counselling sourcebook: A practical reference on contemporary issues*. Crossroad Publishing, New York, 362-386.

Ryan, M. P., & Ryan, J. J. (1967). *Love and sexuality: A Christian approach*. Winston Limited, New York, 362-380.

Martin, R. (1978). *Husbands, wives, parents, children: Foundations for a Christian family*. Servant Books, Michigan, 31-53.

Lessor, R. (1982). *A transactional analysis and gestalt approach to marriage: Love and marriage*. Argus Communication, New York, 19-40.

Janus, S. S., & Janus, C. L. (1993). *The Janus report on sexual behavior*. Wiley Publishing, New York, 20-32.

Campbell, S. M. (1983). *The couple's journey: Intimacy as a path to wholeness*. Impact Publishers, California, 6-47.

Thompson, L., & Walker, A. J. (1991). *Gender in families: Women and men in marriage, work, and parenthood*. Minneapolis, 125-137.

Victor, A. (2010). *Journey of a counselor*. Sevasadhan Publishing, Bangalore, 52-55.

Sills, D. L., & Merton, R. K. (Eds.). (1975). *International encyclopedia of the social sciences*. The Macmillan Company & the Free Press, New York.

Kuper, A., & Kuper, J. (Eds.). (1985). *The social science encyclopedia*. Routledge, London